A Family
at Law

A Family at Law

In which the Henderson family
finds out what to do after an accident

Douglas Stewart
and
Gavin Campbell
Illustrated by **William Rushton**

Fourmat Publishing

ISBN 1 85190 044 6

First published September 1988

The characters in this book are entirely fictitious and
are not intended to bear any resemblance to any person
living or dead.

© Douglas Stewart and Gavin Campbell
Published by Fourmat Publishing
27 & 28 St Albans Place Islington Green London N1 0NX
Printed in Great Britain

Foreword
by Esther Rantzen

This book is the map we have all longed for, through the terrifying jungle of the law. Most of us dread ever having to set foot in that jungle without snake-boots and a very large bullet-proof wallet. Jungle natives speak a language of their own, bristling with strange sounds, "Whereases" and "Heretofores". Even if the path ahead of us looks smooth and straight, there are hidden swamps, like legal costs, to trap us, and lurking dragons, like expert witnesses, to eat us alive. So even injured people who urgently need and richly deserve the compensation that a court could award, may still prefer not to venture inside the legal jungle. After all, there are those who disappear and are never seen again. Jungle safaris are usually only for the very rich, the very brave, or the extremely stubborn.

This book cuts away the tangled creepers, tames the dragons, interprets the language, allows us to explore the jungle with confidence. It provides realistic practical information, and excellent advice. The two authors come from widely different backgrounds. Gavin Campbell, my colleague on BBC TV's *"That's Life"* is an actor and producer, and also an investigative journalist. Douglas Stewart is a lawyer who is particularly distinguished by his campaigning concern for those who suffer injury and need recompense. They have proved themselves to be a most effective team. Gavin Campbell interviewed for the programme *"Children of Courage"*, a nine-year-old boy grievously disabled in a motor accident. It was clear to him that the family had been shattered by the tragedy, not only because the child had been paralysed, but also because they were suffering such grinding poverty that his mother had to work full-time, and even so was not able to adapt their home for his needs, buy him the special aids he needed, or obtain a place for him at the right school. In spite of all the hurdles, the boy was fighting with extraordinary courage to walk again, and was beginning to succeed. Gavin believed the law could and should support this family. He alerted Douglas Stewart, and once Douglas had learned the facts of the case, and began to fight for them, the picture changed dramatically. Douglas knew they had a strong case for compensation, and he won it for them. Now they have the means to buy and adapt a bungalow, and pay for special schooling. Money cannot bring back the little boy's health and strength, but it has allowed him to harness that extraordinary courage and persistence, and it has provided his family with the means to help him. If any reader needs proof that the advice in this book works, I can assure you I have seen that proof.

Not all the fictitious cases in this book are tragic; this is a most entertaining guide. Lawyers will be given plenty to think about in these pages—the book begins and ends with the same overriding advice, "The most important decision you make is which solicitor to appoint—don't get it wrong." Up to now it has been difficult for the consumer to judge a lawyer; read this book and you will have standards to judge them by, and your own strong thread to guide you safely through the legal jungle.

Esther Rantzen
June 1988

Preface

A Family At Law is intended to be an amusing book about the law. But it is also serious because it sets out to unravel the confusion and fear often experienced after an accident, a medical mistake or similar personal misfortune. In it we follow the fictitious Henderson family who are smitten with a series of disasters, each of which highlights different compensation claims and how they should be pursued.

It is a sad statistical fact that you or someone you know will be seriously injured. Whether or not this has happened, *A Family at Law* will help you cope when the luck runs out. But even where the law can help, input is needed from the victim, his friends and relatives. This book will help you to help yourself.

It is not a text book containing a complete explanation of the law relating to accidents, but gives broad guidance on the topics covered. Advice on a particular case should always be obtained from a suitably qualified solicitor.

A Family At Law is based on the law in England and Wales. In Scotland, similar laws apply, but they are not exactly the same. Some Acts of Parliament apply to England and Wales *and* Scotland; some to Scotland only and some to England and Wales only. English and Scottish law vary fundamentally in some respects, but in the field of accident claims, there are many similarities. The "common law" rules, which make up the law of negligence in England and Wales, and the law of delict in Scotland, are broadly similar.

Much of this book concerns choice of solicitors, tactics and how to help yourself, all of which are fundamental on both sides of the border. Where there are important differences, they are pointed out in the text.

We would like to thank Andrew Spink, Barrister–at–Law, and Duncan White, Sheriff Clerk at Edinburgh, for their helpful recommendations; Esther Rantzen for her enthusiasm and encouragement; and Penny Stewart for coping so ably with the typing.

Douglas Stewart
Gavin Campbell

London
1988

Contents

The Henderson Family

Our "family at law" are the Hendersons. Arthur and Jackie Henderson are married and live in Croydon in South London. At the beginning of our story, Arthur is forty-three years old and Jackie is thirty-eight. He is a warehouse manager. She works part time in a department store. Living with them are their three children, Wayne, aged nineteen, Katie aged nine, and Susie, six. Also living in the household is Arthur's mother, Martha Henderson - a peppery seventy-one year old.

Life has been kind to the Hendersons, but now their luck is running out. Each one of them has to pursue a claim for compensation. First it is Arthur . . .

For Michael Beeforth, whose unfailing courage and humour are an inspiration to us all.

Choosing
a
Solicitor

in which Arthur gets it wrong

Cursing under his breath, Arthur Henderson struggled on his crutches into the High Street offices of Messrs Hedge, Fudgitt and Ponder. Lying in hospital, the chap in the next bed had told him that he had a good claim for the nasty injuries he had received in his road accident and had recommended that Arthur saw his solicitor. Arthur hadn't given much thought to choosing a solicitor but he'd dealt with old Will Ponder (William Torquil Ponder, to give him his full name) before, the fat chap with the round face and big black glasses, who'd done the conveyancing when he'd moved house a few years previously. He'd done that well enough and anyway it was comforting to be able to go back to the same office and to get advice from someone he knew.

Would things have changed he wondered as he opened the frosted glass door? He was reassured. Nothing had changed. All the familiar sights of the dingy waiting room greeted him, as did Mr Ponder's receptionist. Doris, with her pre-War typewriter, seemed almost pre-War herself. She had barely changed since Arthur had last seen her—still wearing an old-fashioned cardigan and a resigned, careworn look. If she had ever hoped for a handsome prince to sweep her away from the cobwebs and faded files, she had surely given up by now.

'Do sit down, Mr Henderson. Mr Ponder won't keep you a moment.' Doris nodded towards a battered armchair. Lowering himself into the chair carefully, Arthur grimaced as an aggressive spring attacked him through the upholstery. Fancy forgetting that spring! Ah! Something had changed! There was a new magazine. *Now* there was a choice of *Woman's Own* or *Pigeon Fanciers' Almanac*. He'd just decided to plump for the pigeons when the round shape of the solicitor appeared.

Arthur gets it wrong

'Please come in Mr Henderson,' croaked Mr Ponder who seemed to have developed a list to starboard over the years. Arthur wondered if it was a touch of gout from the Rotary Club port. In the hush of Mr Ponder's office, dust lay thick on the Last Will and Testament of Emily Braithwaite, but on Ponder's desk nothing seemed to have moved over the intervening years. The papers were as well organized as an army in retreat.

'I've read your letter. So you've had an accident. Most unfortunate,' muttered Mr Ponder. 'Very difficult, very hard to succeed in this sort of claim. Expensive too. Needs careful handling. Nothing as uncertain as a court case. Funny people, judges.' He fell silent for what seemed an eternity, hands on his stomach, playing with his watch chain. 'Definitely one to think about.' His chins wobbled in agreement with his observations.

'But a friend told me I had a good case. I was on the main road. The other chap shot out from a side turning.' Arthur's voice was a touch shrill and nervously he patted down his unruly bush of hair which he'd neatly parted down the middle for the occasion. Mr Ponder tapped the side of his nose knowingly, dislodging a crumb from his moustache as he did so. 'Don't listen to people who don't understand the law. You take my advice. Accident claims. Uncharted territory. Could take years to get to court. Insurers are difficult. Very.'

'How much will it cost then?'

'Shouldn't care to say.' Mr Ponder wasn't sure anyway. 'Thousands maybe. Could be a long time in court. It's not easy getting money out of insurers— they deny everything. Very tricky.' The look on his face suggested to Arthur that it was downright bloody impossible.

3

Arthur shifted uncomfortably and stared at the carpet. From the walls, cartoons of decaying judges leered their contempt at him. 'Well, how much is it worth?'

'Broken leg? Could be a lot of money. I can remember getting . . . ooh . . . £500 for a chap with a broken leg once. Never forget it. 1961 it was. Good year for claret. Mind, he was younger than you. Your claim may not be worth as much.' Ponder thought for a moment. Yes. He'd covered himself against getting the client over-optimistic. Right. Musn't scare the chap off. 'I think you ought to go ahead with the claim though.' As he nodded his head, once again his chins seemed to confirm that view.

'So you'll take the case on, will you?' Arthur was relieved.

'Oh yes! But I'll need some money on account of costs. A few hundred.'

'But . . . ' Arthur was hesitant. 'What about ALAS?'

'Alas what?'

'ALAS—the new Law Society scheme to help accident victims.' Arthur saw the glazed look on Mr Ponder's face. 'Oh, never mind! I don't suppose it would help me. What about legal aid? Or Green Form legal aid?' Arthur had heard about this on the telly.

Mr Ponder coughed politely. 'I hope you're not trying to tell me my job Mr . . . er . . . Mr. The Green Form Scheme really wouldn't help you in this situation. And I don't suppose you're eligible for legal aid. Good Heavens no.' He looked at Arthur's letter. 'Let me see,' he prevaricated. 'You've been earning £12,000 a year. With that type of income there's no chance. So what I suggest is that you pay me £350 on account of costs, but I shall need more from time to time—to stoke the boilers so to speak.'

'£350,' mused Arthur. 'That's hard to come by but I'll raise it somehow. If you really think that I can win.'

'No guarantees. Very difficult. But I think you should go ahead.'

Mr Ponder moved to show out his client. 'Delighted to act for you.' In the baggy shapeless suit he'd bought for his father's funeral in 1969, William Torquil Ponder extended his pudgy paw to his client. With familiar ease he sidestepped three tin boxes full of old deeds written in those glorious days when solicitors were paid by the word. 'Well . . . I'll be hearing from you then er . . . Mr . . . er Anderson,' concluded Mr Ponder in satisfaction, as his client struggled to free one of his crutches from a hole in the Axminster carpet.

After the gloom of Ponder's office, Arthur had to blink as he emerged into the High Street, even though it was a winter's evening. As he was hovering by the foot of the steps, he had his first lucky break. 'Arthur, good to see you.' It was PC Smethers, who had been a neighbour over twenty years before. 'Been getting old Ponder to make your Will? I can see you've had an accident but surely you're not that far gone? Not just yet anyway.'

Arthur smiled uncertainly. 'Had a bit of a dust-up. Stupid blighter pulled out in front of me. Wrote my car off. *And* I'd only polished it that morning. So I was instructing Mr Ponder to deal with the accident claim.'

'You were what!' The policeman's helmet almost fell off as he rocked with laughter. 'That's a joke for a start. That man's one big accident. If you want compensation, don't go near him. Kiss of death. Don't get me wrong. If you want a Will made or are selling your house, old Ponder'll get it right. No Arthur, if you've got an accident claim you've got to see a specialist solicitor. Getting money out of insurers is a bit of a war. Any insurance claims man would tie old Ponder into so many knots that he'd think it was bondage night in Bangkok. Take my tip. Go and see Paul Bright. He's only just down the road and he specialises in compensation cases. He'll see you right.'

'Thanks. I'll do that.'

There are two morals to this story:

- If you have an accident claim, find a specialist solicitor (see below).

- Find a solicitor with whom you can feel comfortable and in whom you have real faith.

Finding an accident claims specialist:

Some Do's and Don'ts and the reasons why

There are a number of ways in which you can help yourself. By making a little extra effort at the beginning, you can dramatically improve your chances of success. Here are some do's and don'ts.

- DO think of friends or relatives who may have made a claim for damages. Ask if they were happy with their solicitor, and then meet the solicitor to form your own view.

- DO, if you are a member of a trade union, ask the local officers if they can recommend someone.

- DO ask The Law Society at 113 Chancery Lane, London WC2. They can give you the names of firms, as can the Secretary of the Local Law Society for your area. Feel free to consult each of them before making a choice and then follow the other guidance in this chapter.

- DO visit a Crown Court. Most cities and major towns have one. Look under 'Courts' in the telephone directory. Find out whether they take what are called 'civil' cases, because your claim comes into that category. On display at such courts will be a list of the cases awaiting trial and by looking down the names of the firms of solicitors you will see which firms keep on appearing in the civil cases. From this you will establish:

  — which solicitors handle the right type of case;

— that they fight things as far as bringing them on for trial. Many don't, through inexperience.

Look for the solicitors who are representing 'plaintiffs' because most plaintiffs are claiming damages. Solicitors listed as acting for 'defendants' are usually representing insurance companies who are picking up the bill for the person who is being sued. However, just because a firm appears regularly in the list as acting for defendants does not mean that they will not act for someone like you. Indeed they may be an ideal choice (see below).

- DO ask the solicitor at the very beginning whether the interview is under the new 'ALAS' scheme which gives you thirty minutes of free legal advice on whether you have a valid accident claim to pursue. Find out whether the solicitor will handle your claim on legal aid and if not, ask about charging rates and do not hesitate to ask for the advice to be put in writing.

- DO, whether or not you are having a free half hour with a solicitor under the ALAS scheme, get the most from the interview by jotting down in advance the basic facts which the solicitor will want to know. (These basic facts are set out on page 29).

- DO, when you meet the solicitor, ask about:

  — the number of claims which he or she has handled and how much of his or her time is taken up with claims.

  — the size and number of cases he or she has

actually fought in court. Many solicitors for claimants are inexperienced and have never got a case to court. Too frequently they settle cases too cheaply rather than risk going to court.

- DON'T rely on solicitors' advertisements alone. Many of the best specialists have no need to advertise. Many of the emptiest legal vessels make the most sound.

- DON'T pick a firm of solicitors with a pin when looking at Yellow Pages or similar directory.

- DON'T assume that a firm which you see described (perhaps in a directory) as undertaking damages/compensation claims is necessarily right for you. Many firms register willingness to take on just about anything. Use the directories as a useful signpost.

- DON'T appoint the solicitor at the first interview if you have any doubts. With a basic three year time limit for making claims of this type, you can normally afford to look around. You can change your solicitor at a later stage, but it may be difficult, expensive and embarrassing (see page 15).

- DON'T be impressed by solicitors like Mr Ponder who give you an instant value of the claim on inadequate information and without knowing the medical situation.

- DON'T feel frightened or nervous about consulting a solicitor. Good ones will quickly put you at ease and most of them are almost human, sharing your interests in the local football or cricket team, holidays, tennis or whatever. If the solicitor you consult is a pompous ass cut loose at once! (see page 15).

(see page 15)

THE MOST IMPORTANT DECISION YOU MAKE IS WHICH SOLICITOR TO APPOINT - DON'T GET IT WRONG.

Here are some very good reasons for taking the trouble to find the right solicitor at the start:

- He or she has the first chance to determine policy and tactics. The wrong decision at the beginning can ruin a good case within minutes.

- Your solicitor has to take the initiatives and make things happen. A bad solicitor lets events overtake him or her.

- He or she has to choose the best counsel (barrister or, in Scotland, advocate) to represent you if the case goes to court. Only a specialist will know which counsel will make the best job of your case.

- Your solicitor chooses and instructs medical witnesses and other experts, including engineers, rehabilitation specialists or employment specialists. An experienced claims solicitor knows who the real experts are, and who are the best people to have on your side.

- He or she carries on negotiations with insurers or their solicitors. Most cases are settled by negotiation. Obviously, the more experienced your negotiator, the better the settlement you are likely to get. A bad solicitor may have no idea of the value of the claim and may abdicate responsibility to a barrister who, in turn, may not have been wisely chosen.

Changing
your
solicitor

in which Arthur has a nightmare

Arthur shifted uncomfortably, his face clearly demonstrating his agony. 'But please, Mr Ponder, I've decided to change my solicitor, I want you to send all my papers round to Paul Bright.'

'Change solicitors?' Mr Ponder's moustache bristled in menace and the colour in his cheeks deepened to burgundy. William Torquil Ponder was most indignant as he recalled the work he'd done over the years. His voice rasped at this treachery. 'You can't do that. We've got an agreement. I'm acting for you. Quite unreasonable. Impossible. Hedge, Fudgitt and Ponder have always acted for your family.'

Arthur quivered in his seat. From behind Ponder's head, the portrait of the late Oliver Hedge in his General's uniform added menace. The eyes seemed to challenge Arthur to defy Mr Will Ponder at his peril. 'I'm sorry. I've made up my mind. I do want to change. Anyway, we didn't agree anything.'

'Very well then. If you insist. But it will be costly. I shall have to charge you for my time for the first interview, for reading your papers and now for this meeting.' He fondled the last tufts of hair just above his whiskery ears. 'I shall have to think about it most carefully but, if your were to pay, say £150, I think that would probably cover it.'

'What! £150. That's a bit steep.'

'Plus VAT of course. I'm afraid if you won't pay me, then I have my solicitor's lien on your papers. I shall have to exercise it. That means I won't release your papers to anyone until I'm paid. I suggest you make up your mind as quickly as possible. Every minute is costing you money. Just look at the clock.'

The ringing in Arthur's ears awakened him. 'Stop the clock Mr Ponder, stop the clock!' he shouted.

'Do be quiet Arthur,' chided Jackie, his wife,

sitting up sharply in bed. 'Whatever's the matter? It's only the alarm clock. It's time to get up.'

'Thank goodness for that. I was dreaming. I was sure I was in Mr Ponder's office.'

'No. Don't you remember. You're going to consult Paul Bright.'

'So I was. I've got an appointment with him today.'

Changing solicitors need not be a nightmare

If you want to change solicitors, remember the following points:

- Do it quickly. The longer you put it off the more difficult it gets.

- If you change your solicitor, the old one is entitled to be paid for work *properly* done.

- A solicitor does have a *lien*—a legal right to retain your papers as security for unpaid fees—but only for *proper* fees for work *properly* done.

If a solicitor wrongfully exercises a lien, ie keeps your papers but is overcharging or has given bad advice—then the solicitor will be liable to you for damages for wrongful retention of your papers if this causes you loss.

If you want to change solicitors for good reason, most solicitors will co-operate. If the old solicitor, like Ponder in the nightmare, makes life difficult, it is often because he or she suspects that another solicitor will consider their work sub-standard or negligent. Furthermore, on request, The Law Society can investigate what is a proper fee (if any) for shoddy work and your new solicitor can advise what redress you may have if the work was positively *negligent*.

If you cannot face the solicitor you wish to dismiss, then give written authority to your new solicitor to take up the cudgels for you.

If you cannot afford to pay the charge demanded, then your new solicitor should be able to persuade the first solicitor to accept an undertaking to clear the *proper* costs out of any damages and costs you win in the end. Also, if your new solicitor can definitely identify shortcomings in the legal advice given, or genuinely question the amount of charges raised, then again there should be no problem in getting the papers transferred. On receiving the papers your new solicitor can tell you whether the advice was correct and whether the charges were reasonable and, if not, what should be done about it.

The relationship between solicitor and client is based on mutual confidence. Solicitors cannot stop acting for you without good reason. Similarly you should not change your solicitor unless that mutual confidence has broken down. This is particularly important if you are legally aided. (Legal aid is dealt with in the next chapter.) A legally aided person *can* change solicitors. However, the legal aid authorities look closely at any request to do so because they know that some clients are unreasonable. If they are satisfied that mutual confidence *has* broken down, they normally permit a change of solicitors. Indeed (with increasing reluctance) they sometimes sanction several changes. Your new solicitor will explain to the legal aid authorities why you want to change. If your original solicitor was glad to see the back of you, then he or she will also inform The Law Society that mutual confidence no longer exists. Only if the old solicitor puts in a report saying that you are being unreasonable might you run into difficulties, but usually the client is given the benefit of the doubt, at least on the first occasion.

If you change solicitors, there is bound to be some duplication of work as your new solicitor reads what has gone on before. This may be at your expense or at the expense of the legal aid fund; or, if the first solicitor was negligent, then an indemnity might be claimed against that solicitor for the cost of work done to no advantage, together with the damages. It is unlikely that the cost of duplication can be recovered from the insurers on the other side.

Any expense in changing solicitors is almost invariably worthwhile if you have made a mistake in your first choice. Bad advice from the wrong solicitor can cost you dearly in damages and can lose you the case.

ONCE AGAIN: THE SINGLE MOST IMPORTANT FACTOR IN ACCIDENT CLAIMS LITIGATION IS HAVING THE RIGHT SOLICITOR. A BAD SOLICITOR CAN RUIN A GOOD CASE.

Paying
for
it
all

in which Arthur meets Paul Bright, an
accident claims specialist

'Real space-age this,' thought Arthur Henderson, as he sat in the waiting room of Messrs Bright and Keen. A photocopier was busy, as were three people typing furiously with TV screens in front of them. More like Jodrell Bank than a solicitors' office. 'What's that then?' he enquired of a trim young secretary who was looking at a small box from which sheets of paper were suddenly emerging as if by magic.

'That's our Fax machine. These documents coming through are being fed into a similar machine at this moment in Manchester but the copies come out here, in Croydon High Street. I can then send copies to Manchester of Mr Bright's letters in reply. Or to anywhere. New York even. Saves time and postage. We've got Telex too, but Fax is the way ahead. Don't know what we did without it.' The young woman smiled warmly at him as she answered the phone by her side. 'Ah! Mr Bright's ready to see you now. I'll show you in.'

'Good Morning Mr Henderson.' Mr Bright, a solicitor aged thirty-four and well groomed, rose from his desk. 'I expect you'd like a cup of coffee. I'll get that organized while we talk about your accident. Sounds rather nasty from what you told me over the phone.' His desk was tidy, the room lined with filing cabinets and no clutter or Ponder-like confusion in sight.

'White with no sugar, thanks.' Arthur Henderson sat down and made instant comparisons between the dusty wasteland of Mr Ponder's office and the neat stacks of files lying beside Mr Bright's desk. The room was tidy, comfortable, well-organized, with just the right balance of law books and personal knick-knacks to be interesting.

'As you know, I've been recommended to you,' Arthur volunteered diffidently. 'But having seen all

19

your technology out there, I'm worried about what it's all going to cost. Are you very expensive? Can I afford to use you? I hope you don't mind me asking that first.'

Mr Bright laughed. 'Not at all. Let's clear that straight away. You're quite right. Someone has to pay for all the technology. My aim with claims such as yours is to make sure it's the insurers who pick up the tab. Can't guarantee it of course, so let's just look at the possibilities.'

'I've heard about the ALAS scheme. What's that?'

'Good place to start. That's the Accident Legal Advice Service. You'll have seen the 'thumbs-up' sticker in our window, no doubt. I can give you half an hour of free advice and tell you whether or not your claim is worth pursuing. The Law Society introduced the scheme because so many people don't bother to pursue their accident claims at all. It's far better than the previous scheme which was the fixed-fee interview —better for you, that is, because it's free. Under the fixed-fee scheme, at least I got £5! But most solicitors are pleased with ALAS. It gets more people like you coming through the door to find out whether their claim is worth pursuing. So let's assume that this meeting is under the ALAS scheme, shall we?'

'Might as well save the £5,' Arthur replied. He liked the man. There was a straightforward sense of purpose about him.

'All right then,' said Paul Bright, with a grin. 'I'll just have to put off the Rolls Royce for a while. Once the half hour runs out, we can move on to the legal aid green form scheme if you are financially eligible. With that I can do £50 worth of work and sometimes I can get the £50 figure extended.'

'How much does the green form scheme cost then?'

'Well, if you're on Income Support or have Family Income Supplement, then you are immediately eligible. It's free. Otherwise I can do a quick check on your family finances and work out how much it's going to cost. All you need to know is that it's good value. I have to find out how much you and your wife bring in, what dependants you have. From that I can work out whether you have to contribute say £5 or £15 in order to buy £50 or more of advice.'

'I don't suppose £50 goes far, does it?'

'Fraid not but I can deal with the ground-work. I'd be able to put together the basic facts which you'll need in your legal aid application. That's different from the green form scheme. Rather more complicated but of great help in a claim of this sort.'

'I'm still being paid by my employers. Jackie, that's my wife, also has a job. I should think between us we bring in more than £16,000 a year. I've got three children. Do you think I'm eligible for legal aid?'

'I don't think you'll scrape into the green form scheme but, if you've got a mortgage and other financial outgoings like life insurance premiums, then it's certainly worth submitting an application for legal aid proper. Let's look at that after I've heard all about your accident.'

'Fine, but I was reading about some new fixed costs scheme. Will that help me?'

Mr Bright shook his head. 'Not yet. It hasn't been introduced. If it does come in, then it could be a great help to accident victims. You'll simply make a one-off payment which will enable me to fight your entire case. If you lose, then it costs only what you paid at the beginning. If you win, you still don't get the money back, but you get your damages in full. My firm would be paid either by the insurers if we win, or by the scheme if we lose. I reckon this idea is going to be a winner.' Mr Bright leant across the desk. 'So make sure you don't have another accident until the new scheme comes in.'

Arthur laughed. 'I'll do my best.'

'Do you have your own legal expenses insurance? By that I mean has anyone ever talked you into taking out your own insurance policy to pay for legal costs. Some household policies even provide this cover as an optional extra. There are various companies such as Hambros, Allianz and DAS. If you've got a policy, then we notify them of your claim and they become responsible for the costs. Unfortunately, not many people have taken these policies out. Have you?'

'No. I'm one of the foolish virgins I suppose.'

'If you're eligible for legal aid then it's not so foolish but the Government has cut eligibility so much that fewer and fewer people can get it. For those not eligible for legal aid then costs are obviously a worrying factor and the policies are worth considering. It'll be interesting to see how these insurers react if The Law Society's fixed costs scheme comes in. At least you don't have to pay premiums year after year. You simply have to be able to pay one lump sum when and if the rainy day comes.'

'That all seems very clear.'

Paul Bright looked at his watch jokingly. 'We've got sixteen minutes left. In that time I've got to be able to advise you whether or not you've got a claim at all.'

'Fine, but if I'm not eligible for the green form, how much will it cost me after the half hour is up?'

'My hourly charging rate is £40. In central London, rather than here in Croydon, charges are considerably more, and a solicitor in mid Wales might be charging rather less. Overheads vary from area to area. However, you must understand that the basic hourly rate is not the final charge because on top of that we are entitled to charge a mark-up depending on various points like the complexity of the matter. In accident cases it's quite likely to be 50% and sometimes more. That means that £40 per hour becomes £60 per hour, which all goes to show that we've got to finish this interview in half an hour so that it's all free.'

'Too right! £60 an hour!'

'But if you ever stop to think of the profit a car dealer makes when you walk into the showroom and drive out in a new Sierra, you might not think that £60 an hour was quite so expensive. Anyway, in this situation you should think positively. If I think your claim is as good as you do, we'll be sending most of the bill to the insurers.'

'Does the winner always get all his costs paid?'

'No. Look, we're running out of time. I'll explain that later. It normally takes six weeks for legal aid to come through and in some areas it's three months now. The delays are infuriating but the country can't afford to appoint the staff to deal with things more quickly. Once you've got legal aid, we can look at all the details to find out what the loser has to pay in damages and costs. Let's look at the accident itself now. Just tell me what happened.'

For the next few minutes Arthur described how he'd been driving along the main road, at a proper speed, in daylight, keeping a proper look-out, when a car suddenly emerged from a side road on his left. A collision had been inevitable, and Paul Bright was immediately able to advise that, on this version of events, there would be no difficulty in getting legal aid on the merits of the case if Arthur were financially eligible. 'This looks to me like a strong case and one where, if the insurers do not pay up, then we can take them all the way to court if need be.'

Paul Bright then quickly checked Arthur's financial situation and found that he was too well off for the green form scheme. 'You're now paying for my time but hopefully the insurers will pay in the end. Let's fill in these two blue legal aid forms which I send off. The circumstances of your accident are then checked to see if you have a good case, which you do. Secondly your financial circumstances are investigated by the DHSS. They get in touch with you and ask all sorts of impertinent questions like, how many Swiss bank accounts do you have and was the photograph on the mantelpiece of Grandma taken by Lord Snowdon and therefore incredibly valuable.'

'You mean they might take my life savings?'

'Yes.' Paul Bright smiled impishly. 'It pays to be a spendthrift, doesn't it? If you've got disposable capital of more than about £4,850, then they'll expect you to use that first before they grant legal aid. That's the general rule.'

'Well, I've only got about £450 in premium bonds.'

'You won't have any problem then. Anyway, so far as income goes, your *disposable* income must be less than £5,585 a year. Passing through the eye of this needle is getting increasingly difficult because of Government cutbacks. Basically the DHSS look at your income and your wife's income and tot that up. They then make deductions for all your dependants, and regular and proper commitments, and if that figure ends up less than £5,585, then you get legal aid. If it ends up lower than £2,325 a year, it costs you nothing and between those figures you have to pay a contribution spread over twelve months.'

'So I might have to pay something towards legal aid by the sound of it.'

'Yes, but if you get legal aid you're lucky. It's a marvellous weapon. It doesn't suit me too well because on a High Court case such as yours will be, not only can I not charge at a fair rate for my overheads, but also 5% of my proper costs are withheld and put into the legal aid fund to keep it going. Added to that, I get burdened with a mass of bureaucracy, but for you, a legal aid certificate gives you peace of mind in knowing that your own costs are not a worry and, except in circumstances which need not trouble you, you don't pick up the other side's bill even if the case is lost.' Paul Bright's friendly face smiled conspiratorially. 'This means that insurers have a great incentive to settle.'

'That sounds attractive. Part of the better news you've given me.' Arthur sipped his cold coffee thoughtfully. 'And if I win? Do I keep all my damages?'

'Maybe, but probably not all of them. Nearly all of them. Any costs which the other side doesn't pay, which leaves the legal aid fund out of pocket, are recouped from your damages. But in a case the size of yours, where you've got serious injuries, this really is nothing to worry about. You'll have to rely on my judgement.'

'Fine,' Arthur nodded contentedly. What a difference from Old Ponder! Paul Bright was just the sort you needed when you were in a jam. You could see that he would stand no nonsense from insurers. Nor from anyone.

'OK, I'll fill the forms in. Let's hope I'm lucky.'

'If you're not eligible for legal aid, we'll work out how best to fund your court case. I expect you've read figures in newspapers about what this sort of thing costs. Take no notice. It's all press talk. Wildly inaccurate rubbish usually! All you need to know at the moment is that over 90% of these cases are settled during negotiations. Normally I would expect to get damages for you plus my firm's costs on top. If I can't get my costs in full, then I am entitled to deduct proper costs from your damages but it wouldn't make much of a dent in a claim as big as this.'

'Insurers don't necessarily pay the costs in full?'

'No, because the law doesn't order them to. They pay what are called standard costs, which don't necessarily amount to a complete indemnity. To my mind it's crazy but it's the law. Certainly, if you don't have legal aid, I would be entitled to charge you something on top of what I recover by way of costs from the other side. Whether I do so would depend on the circumstances at that time.'

'I haven't had anything by way of State handouts. Should I have?'

'Yes. There'll be a lot of grilling and form-filling but get down to the DHSS as soon as you can. They'll sort it out. You've been missing out but I expect they will backdate your entitlement.'

'Thanks. It would be nice to get something back from the Government for a change.'

The interview was over and Paul Bright closed the file. Arthur struggled to his feet, slung his satchel over his shoulder and prepared to leave. 'It's like being back at school again, having to wear a satchel. Just one of those funny things you have to do when you're on crutches and can't carry things. But I'm getting used to the stairs now. Oh, there was something else I wanted to ask. If I don't get legal aid, can I do a deal with you so that if I lose the case I pay nothing and if I win you take an agreed share of the damages?'

'If I did that sort of deal with you I'd be hauled up by The Law Society and expelled. I'd end my days publishing books in Islington. [It is not, of course, true to suggest that publishers employ struck-off solicitors. The publishers wished to delete this sentence, but authors will have their little joke!—Ed.] In America they allow it. It might happen here one day. There's talk about it.'

Paul Bright followed his client into the corridor, carefully noting the way he walked, heavily reliant on his crutches. 'Besides legal aid delays, there'll be all types of delay while I fight your case. Most of it beyond my control.'

Arthur laughed. 'I've heard about the law's delays.' He felt relaxed, light-headed even. No touch of the Ponders here. 'Next you'll be telling me that solicitors never delay things.'

Paul Bright grinned and pointed his client towards the front door. 'Any more remarks like that and you might find that you're getting serious pains in your good leg.' He stood by the door, all six foot two inches of him. 'Joking apart, I'll certainly explain about the law's delays some time.'

The morals of this story are:

- Ask questions. See how much Arthur Henderson learned about costs and legal aid in just a few minutes.

- Do get the most out of the free half hour. Have your basic facts (see below) jotted down. It's always difficult to remember everything at a single meeting, especially if you're nervous. Better still, if you can let the solicitor have the basic facts, briefly and concisely in the post before the meeting, even more progress can be made in that short half hour.

- Do have an idea of your financial circumstances. Better still, jot them down so that quick decisions can be taken about whether you are likely to be eligible for legal aid.

- Note than in Scotland things are a little different; legal aid is administered by the Scottish Legal Board. There is no ALAS in Scotland, but accident victims are helped under the "Pink Form Scheme". Otherwise, legal aid in Scotland is much the same as in England and Wales.

Basic facts checklist

Experience shows that most people, on first instructing a solicitor, forget vital points. To help yourself, to save time and therefore expense, it is well worth writing down the following information which your solicitor will need at the first meeting. If some of the information is not available, don't put off the interview. If you are not able to write it down, then at least have as many of the answers as possible in mind.

The following basic information will be required by your solicitor in *all* accident cases:

- your full names, date of birth and occupation;

- your address and telephone number;

- if you think you may need financial assistance, broad details of your income, capital and expenses (such as rent or mortgage), including those of your spouse;

- if you have ever had legal aid before, details of the legal aid number and what it was for;

- address of any office from which you receive State benefits, such as Income Support or Industrial Injury Benefit, and your National Insurance number;

- the name and address of your doctor;

- the name and address of any hospital attended, with the names of any doctors/specialists who examined you;

29

- details of any income lost;

- details of any expenses which you have incurred, such as travelling to hospital;

- details of the injuries you have suffered;

- details of any items of property, such as clothing, which may have been lost or damaged;

- details of any legal expenses insurance cover which you may have;

- names and addresses of any witnesses who might help.

The above information is always needed. If your injuries were sustained in a *road* accident, you should also gather together the following:

- the date, time and place of the accident;

- details of any other driver involved, together with details of his or her insurance cover, if possible;

- the name and address of your own insurers and your policy number;

- how the accident occurred and who you blame, wholly or in part;

- whether you were wearing a seat belt and if not, whether you were in a position where a seat belt should have been worn;

- details of the police officer who investigated and the address of the police station most closely involved;

- whether you gave a statement to the police, and if so, whether it is an accurate reflection of what you now believe to be the position;

- whether you or anyone else took photographs of the accident spot or vehicles; who took them and when;

- location of the vehicle now and whether or not it has been repaired;

- whether or not there is likely to be any visible sign such as skid marks or debris still at the scene of the accident which might be helpful to prove who was to blame;

- if you have no personal recollection of the accident, the source of your information;

- the state of the weather and street lighting if the accident occurred after dark; and any special characteristics of the accident spot which you think are relevant.

Bring to the meeting any letters received by you and copies of any letters which you have written relating to the accident. Beware of writing letters to insurers or others involved in the accident until you have taken legal advice, and do keep copies of any letters which you do write. Also bring to the meeting any photographs, receipts, notes of expenses and any other papers connected with the accident.

Legal expenses insurance

Arthur was asked if he had legal expenses insurance. Like most people, he did not, yet in Germany this type of cover is almost universal. Slowly it is catching on here. There are specialist schemes and you may find that, under your own household policy, legal expenses cover is available if you pay an additional premium.

Legal expenses insurance works like this. You pay premiums for yourself and/or your family *before* you have any claim. In return for this annual premium, when disaster strikes, you will have anything from £10,000 to £50,000 available, which the insurers will pay to your solicitor for his or her own proper charges, for Counsel and expert evidence and the like to fight your case. The insurance company will also pay the other side's costs up to the total insured figure if you lose.

Legal expenses insurance is an excellent idea, particularly for those who are not eligible for legal aid.

The policies differ but, for example, for an annual premium of £6.00 with Hambro you can have cover against the cost of going to law up to £25,000 for motor claims. If you compare that sum with the actual cost of what you would pay for just one hour of a solicitor's time if you are not eligible for legal aid, then it is immediately obvious that legal expenses insurance is as prudent and sensible as having insurance cover on your own home. The fact that you've never had an accident or a need to consult a solicitor makes it statistically more likely that your luck must run out some time.

Study the various schemes, what they cost, what they cover and then decide which is the best for you. Here are the names and addresses of the companies which specialise in legal expenses insurance:

Allianz Legal Protection
Merchants House
Wapping Road
Bristol BS1 4RW
Tel: (0272) 299899

DAS Legal Expenses Insurance Co Ltd
43 George Street
Croydon CR9 1EH
Tel: (01) 680 9564

Hambro Legal Protection Ltd
Hambro House
East Hill
Colchester
CO1 2QN
Tel: (0206) 870570

State Benefits

·NEW CLAIMANTS·

KitKa

in which Arthur pays a visit to the DHSS
but the DHSS doesn't pay much to
Arthur

Bethesda House was eight floors of stalinist utilitarian architecture which dominated the surrounding streets and spoke of faceless and impenetrable bureaucracy. The legends 'Department Of Health And Social Security' and 'Supplementary Benefit', set in brass on the outside of the building, sent a shiver of apprehension up Arthur's spine, as he limped painfully up the worn concrete staircase. Passing a long queue of worn-looking claimants on the first floor landing, he wondered what on earth he was doing in the DHSS office at all.

'Next!'

Arthur looked around him. Nobody moved. The queue of people seemed aimed at a series of metal grilles, divided by glass screens, marked with alphabetical groupings 'A to E', 'F to J', 'K to O' and so on. He found himself forming a queue all on his own opposite a grille marked: 'New Claimants'. It was from behind this grille that the disembodied voice barked again:

'Next!'

Arthur fancied he detected a note of irritation in the voice. He stared blankly at the metal grille.

'I said: Next!'

Arthur looked round at the sea of dejected faces.

'Next!'

This time there was no mistaking the withering tone. It was clearly aimed straight at him. Slowly, gingerly, painfully, Arthur shuffled over the grey lino to the metal grille and sat at the green formica counter in front of it. Through the grille he could just make out a face gleaming venomously at him:

'Yes?!'

The words stabbed out, as Arthur searched through his pockets for the slip of paper with all the questions he would need to ask and answer, written down.

He lowered his head to look into his inside jacket pocket and immediately stabbed himself in the eye with the stem of his pipe poking out of his breast pocket. The sting of the nicotine-coated pipe stem was excruciating. A large tear formed in his eye and rolled slowly down his cheek.

'Yes? . . . Can I help you?'

The contempt on the clerk's face said it all:

'Don't try it on here, Old Son. I've seen 'em all— weepers, moaners, screamers, fainters. It doesn't cut any ice here, so get on and state your claim.'

Arthur's rummaging hand suddenly closed on something deep in the recesses of his pocket. Propelled into speech by this unexpected piece of good fortune, he launched into a stammered falsetto account of his accident and subsequent lay-off at work, resulting in his appearance at the DHSS office today:

' . . . Not my fault . . . Employer very sorry . . . Hospital most sympathetic . . . Doctor very hopeful . . . Full recovery . . . Just a matter of time . . . Wife distraught . . . Kids so grown up about it . . . Solicitor eager to move . . . Bank so very helpful . . . Until now, that is . . . Funds so short . . . Hard to know where it all goes . . . Wouldn't have bothered . . . But . . .'

With a gleam of triumph, Arthur produced his precious piece of paper.

With a look that would have vaporized the Koh-I-Noor Diamond, the clerk examined minutely the crumpled Kit-Kat wrapper from Arthur's pocket. Then, with reptilian ease, he smiled and hissed:

'That's not going to get us very far is it sir? Perhaps we should start again?'

A first visit to the heart of the State benefit bureaucracy can be bewildering. Whilst Arthur's unhappy first taste of the system under the impersonal scrutiny of its guardians is not necessarily typical, it is, regrettably, by no means unusual. Prospective first-time claimants need to have both their wits and their courage about them. They also need to be organised.

As Arthur found out in the end, he was eligible for State support since the accident. As far as the DHSS is concerned, you must help yourself. If you cannot cope with the paper work, get a friend or relative to help. It is worth battling through the red tape, because both long and short term financial help is available. Some payments, like unemployment benefit and income support (previously known as supplementary benefit), will be offset in full against your damages. Others, like industrial disablement, invalidity benefit and sickness benefit are only partially deducted.

Here are a few hints:

- FIND OUT what the different types of benefit are. Here is a list of the main ones:

  — statutory sick pay — sickness benefit
  — invalidity benefit — severe disablement
  — industrial disable- allowance
    ment allowance — attendance allowance
  — invalid care allo- — mobility allowance
    wance — unemployment benefit
  — vaccine damage — income support
    payments

- ASK YOU EMPLOYERS if they provide any welfare services. The personnel officer may be able to help.

- SEE YOUR TRADE UNION representative—most Unions can advise members about claiming benefit.

- KEEP A DIARY of the events following the accident, noting all expenditure, however trivial; this will help show your needs and establish your claim. It will also greatly aid your solicitor.

- WORK OUT your daily and weekly budget, including everything from fuel bills to food for your pet budgerigar.

- KNOW IN ADVANCE what your savings are; make a list of your Bank and Building Society savings, shares, bonds, savings certificates, unit trusts etc.

- KEEP A POSITIVE ATTITUDE to your claim. You and your family may be entitled to a whole range of benefits as a right, not a privilege. Do not go cap in hand. Remember that you have paid into the system. Now you are seeking a little back, so don't feel apologetic.

- ALWAYS BE CALM and collected and never lose your temper—especially with staff at the DHSS. They do not choose or design the system, they are only there to operate it.

Progressing
the
claim

In which Arthur learns something of the
law and of its delays

It was a beautiful spring morning. Arthur felt cheerful. It would soon be the cricket season, even if he couldn't play, and at last he had his legal aid certificate. Things would really move now! Better still, he was down to only one stick. Goodbye to that satchel! For a moment he paused outside Mr Ponder's office, remembering the dark days of last winter when he had struggled up the steps on two crutches to be given more bad advice in half an hour than most people would have thought possible.

What had drawn him in there? Fear of the unknown. That was it, he decided. He'd gone there because he'd been there before. He'd wanted familiarity. Now, without a backward glance at Ponder's emporium, he crossed the road and entered Paul Bright's reception to join five other people who were waiting. A nervous-looking man sitting next to him was staring abstractedly at the machine in the corner and probably thinking about the divorce petition which his wife had just served on him.

'That's Fax,' volunteered Arthur, speaking with all the confidence of the expert. 'You can put a document in there and a photograph of it comes out in Manchester, or anywhere.' The trim receptionist who had taught him gave a knowing wink. He was just about to add that what the secretary was looking at was not a television set but the screen of a new *Olivetti* word processor, when Paul Bright called him through.

'Glad to see you're down to just one stick. Mind you, with the time it takes to get legal aid these days, some of my clients with broken legs are dancing like spring lambs by the time it arrives. Anyway, the main thing is that you've got it, even though it is limited to close of pleadings.'

Arthur looked at his documentation. 'I wondered what that meant. Lawyers' jargon.'

'It's a bit pointless in this case. Increasingly rarely, legal aid is granted immediately for people to fight all the way to court. More often it's limited, to be reviewed after each side has put its arguments in writing. That's what it means.'

'Ah! I see,' said Arthur, stretching out to receive a cup of coffee from Paul Bright's secretary. He crossed his legs, the sudden movement causing the swivel chair to turn sharply, so that the coffee slopped down his thigh. 'Sorry about that,' he muttered. 'Always have trouble with chairs,' he said sheepishly.

'Don't worry.' Paul Bright waited for his client to mop himself up. 'Anyway, let me explain just what happens between now and close of pleadings. Following our first meeting I wrote to the other driver holding him responsible for negligence.'

'And you'll tell me what all that legal language means.'

'Negligence is easy. You must prove the other driver owed you a duty to be careful and that he broke that duty which resulted in you suffering damage. In road accidents or whenever you allege negligence, it means that you have to prove that someone else is to blame. If someone else is *not* to blame, then you've got no claim . No blame, no claim. Easy to remember. You were doing less than thirty in a built-up area. The other driver ignored the 'Give Way' sign and shot out. Plainly he was to blame. Maybe not 100% but at least to blame. There's no suggestion he'd had a heart attack or brake failure. That gives you a valid claim.'

'Glad to hear it, I'm telling you. I didn't stand a chance. How easy is it to prove all this?'

The solicitor eased himself back in the recliner as if preparing himself for a time-worn explanation. It wasn't always easy putting complex legal points into plain language. 'I could bore you rigid with details of the law relating to accidents and evidence. Put simply, it's up to you as the plaintiff, as the person making the claim, to prove your case. You have to show *on the balance of probabilities*, that what happened was the other driver's fault. It doesn't matter if it was partly your fault. That doesn't stop you claiming. It would be useful if there were more witnesses to help prove your viewpoint. Next time make sure that you've got some good witnesses watching!'

Arthur laughed, forgetting for a moment the clammy wetness on his thigh where the coffee was steaming dry. 'I'll try—but I'm not having my next accident before the new fixed cost scheme comes in.' Arthur remembered the advice from before.

Paul Bright smiled in acknowledgement. 'You've got it. Anyway,' he continued, 'I've heard from the insurers for the other driver.

'It's the usual reply, headed "Without Prejudice" and then proceeds to deny everything anyway. The whole purpose of "Without Prejudice" being on letters is to enable the two sides to correspond off the record, with a view to trying to settle a case. However, inexperienced insurance clerks, scared of admitting anything, usually reply "Push off—Without Prejudice", which is what they've said here. In other words, they're saying: "prove to us that we should pay".'

'Does that mean that they don't think they're to blame?'

Paul Bright laughed, leaning backwards and enjoying the moment. 'Forget that idea. No, not at all. Of course, some solicitors take such a denial seriously, but it's just standard insurance tactics. Open admissions of blame are only made in the most obvious of cases and not always even then. If there's a chance of suggesting that you were partly to blame, the insurers can properly take the point. Remember what I said before—it's up to you to prove your case and by making no admissions, the insurers are laying down the rule that they want you to prove everything you allege.'

For the first time that day Arthur felt troubled. 'I wasn't to blame. Just not true.' Arthur's brow furrowed and he ran his hand across his wiry mop of hair.

Bright leant forward across the desk. 'Look. Insurers whistle in the dark. And why shouldn't they, with solicitors like Will Ponder around who take on this sort of work when they know nothing about it. And there's plenty like him. The insurers might well be able to save their shareholders a packet by this sort of denial. Anyway, we have no idea what the other driver told his insurers—maybe a pack of lies.' Paul Bright pointed towards his filing cabinets. 'They're full of cases denied by insurers. I take no notice. I back my own judgement and, for better or worse, you've got to back mine.' He watched as Arthur nodded enthusiastically. 'I'm waiting for the police report. They've decided not to prosecute the other driver. From what *you* tell me, they ought to be prosecuting, but the good news is that I can now get hold of their report.'

'Isn't that bad? That the police are not prosecuting? Doesn't that go against me?'

Paul Bright was emphatic. 'Not at all. I'd rather the police decided not to prosecute than went ahead with a weak case and lost. That would really give the insurers some encouragement, even though what happens in a criminal court is not conclusive in a claim such as yours. A conviction or an admission of guilt is *evidence* of negligence, but doesn't *prove* it. No prosecution at all is merely neutral.'

'That's a relief.' Arthur mopped his brow. His face, never cheerful at the best of times, looked a shade less gloomy. 'I was wondering whether Mr Ponder had been right after all.'

The solicitor's face creased into a friendly laugh before he rose, tall and elegant in a three piece suit of fine cut, and walked to the window. He stared across the busy street at the offices of Hedge, Fudgitt and Ponder. 'Dear old Will Ponder. He really shouldn't try to take on these cases. The first puff of smoke on the horizon and he imagines a posse of Indians is about to arrive. It doesn't pay to dwell on the shortcomings in your own case. Block them up—fine, but the art is in exposing the weaknesses which are worrying the opposition.'

'So I can tell my wife that things are OK?'

'I'm not worried, so you needn't be. If things start to go wrong, I'll tell you quickly enough. It's the insurers who'll be worried. This claim is going to cost them a lot of money. They'll be putting a value on the claim now, and putting pennies in their piggy bank to cover it.'

'Just let me get one thing clear. I always thought that court cases were decided *beyond reasonable doubt*. That's what you always read in the papers.'

'That's because they're dealing with criminal cases. In a claim like this, which is a *civil* claim, however uncivilized some of the people involved might be, it's a lower burden of proof called "on the balance of probabilities", or "more likely than not". Anyway, we must move on to other things. You've kept details of all your expenses, travelling to hospital and so on as I recommended?'

'Yes, here they are.' Arthur handed over a small batch of papers.

'Good. Keep it up. Most important. I know your hobbies were gardening and cricket. We'll have to wait a bit longer to find out how you'll get on with those.'

'My leg's still playing up despite the physio. Gardening will be difficult and cricket looks downright impossible. I was getting a bit past it anyway but I could still move the ball off the seam.'

Paul Bright's face broke into one of his winning smiles. 'Take my advice. Stick to leg breaks.'

Arthur chuckled. 'I'll certainly be fielding at short leg. The specialist says my bad one's one and a half inches shorter than my good one.' Arthur shook with laughter, cup wobbling alarmingly, until, to Paul Bright's relief, he put it down. 'Seriously though, I'll miss this season at least. Do I get compensated for that?'

'Of course. It's part of what we call 'loss of amenities'. We haven't time to deal in detail with damages today. I've instructed a Harley Street consultant called Mr Hacking-Gore to prepare a report on you. Let's wait till I've seen that.' He clasped his hands together as he often did. 'I'm not instructing your surgeon at the local hospital because he's bound to say that he's done a wonderful job.' He shrugged dismissively. 'Which may or may not be true. The medical evidence is vital to my valuation of the claim and that's why it's best to get an independent report. Hacking-Gore may say that your future isn't quite as good as your surgeon had led you to believe. That adds to the value of the claim.'

He handed over two sheets of paper to Arthur. 'Just sign these forms which authorise the hospital and your GP to send their records to Mr Hacking-Gore. He'll need to read these before seeing you and giving an opinion. The bad news is that he's very busy and there'll be some hefty delays. Matter of fact, I got so tired of people blaming me for the law's delays, that I prepared a document which I give to my clients. This sets out all the various parts of the claim and shows where the delay occurs and why it all takes so long.' He slid open a drawer in his desk and handed over a document to Arthur. 'Read this at your leisure. When I've studied the police report I'll be interviewing witnesses and then deciding whether to get a vehicle engineer's report. They can be very useful in persuading judges about angles of impact and speeds of the vehicles. Now, *engineers'* delays are legendary, to the legal profession, if not to the public.' He flourished a hand in Arthur's direction. 'Read all about it.'

'So everyone's to blame but you?'

Paul Bright grinned appreciatively. 'Precisely. You obviously remember my warning about your good leg.'

'Yes—I won't forget that.'

'Anyway I couldn't settle a claim like yours quickly. It can't be resolved until all the effects of your injury are known with reasonable certainty.'

'And when my claim is settled, is that it, once and for all?'

'The answer used to be yes. Now the answer is— not necessarily. There's a new procedure called provisional damages. Insurers hate them. It's a good tactical area. We'll discuss that sort of thing after the medical.'

Arthur shifted in the swivel chair. 'By the way, I start work again next Monday. I'm a bit worried about it. I won't be as fast as I was.'

'Let me know how it goes. It's vital to the value of your claim.'

No blame—no claim

The golden rule in making claims for accident compensation is 'no blame—no claim'. To some extent this has been eroded by Acts of Parliament, but usually, if you are making a claim, you must establish blame. This is the law of *negligence*, and in order to succeed in securing compensation for your damaged vehicle or for your personal injuries, you have to be able to prove:

- that the person you are claiming against owed you a duty to be careful;

- that this person broke that duty and was not careful; and

- that as a result you have suffered damage.

It is because of the complexity of proving these three points that, almost invariably, you need legal advice.

The old common law used to be black and white. If you were free of blame, then you had a claim, but if any blame rested upon you, then you had no claim. Parliament intervened, and the courts are now empowered to apportion blame between the parties. This is the concept of contributory negligence.

Suppose that you are speeding towards a road junction at 40 miles per hour in an area restricted to 30 miles per hour. You are on the main road and the crossroads ahead is wide open, with ample visibility. At the last moment a drunken driver shoots out from the side road into your path so that you collide. You receive serious injuries. How would the law deal with this?

If you were lucky, you might obtain 100% of your damages, but it is more likely that you would have to share the blame. On your behalf it would be argued that your speed was irrelevant; but the chances are it would be said against you that if you had not been speeding you might have had time to avoid the impact. The insurers for the drunken driver would try to split the blame on a fifty-fifty basis and a good solicitor on your behalf would be hoping to get away with a reduction of say 10% for your contributory negligence.

Turning these percentages into mathematics means that, if your claim for damages is worth £10,000, were you free of all blame, then the insurers would be offering 50%, being £5,000, and your own solicitor would be arguing for 90%, being £9,000. If negotiations came to nothing, then a judge would have to determine the issue and you would be stuck with his award.

The golden rule of 'No blame—no claim' applies, for example, in all the following situations:

- negligence by other road users;

- negligence by your doctor;

- negligence by hospitals;

- negligence by your employer (though there may be statutory protection as well);

- negligence by professional people (including solicitors!);

- negligence of animal owners (in some situations);

- negligence of land owners (in some situations).

Normally the task of proving the three elements of negligence (see above) is on the person making the claim. One exception to this is if the facts so obviously imply negligence that the matter can be said to 'speak for itself'. The classic example is the pedestrian who is flattened by a barrel falling from a building. In such circumstances, the claimant can invite the court to reverse the 'burden of proof' so that it is for the person who dropped the barrel to explain, if he can, how it happened without any fault on his part.

Another situation where blame does not have to be proved is where land is put to some unnatural use and something put on the land 'escapes' and causes damage. If your neighbour stores large quantities of inflammables in his garden shed and they then explode, damaging your property, the court will hold your neighbour liable, without your having to prove any blame. Other examples are where the wall of a reservoir bursts and floods your land; or noxious fumes from a chemical plant pollute your land or cause you injury.

Parliament has intervened in some other situations, passing laws to enable claimants to win damages without proving blame. The most important of these are:

- some factory accidents;

- injuries caused by defective products;

- claims arising from the acts of some animals.

It is no longer possible to escape blame for personal injury by denying responsibility at the outset—in a contract for example. Thus, a sign at a skating rink telling skaters that they have no claim for death or personal injury is of no effect. A clause in a document relating to the purchase of a domestic appliance, saying that there is no liability for personal injury, does not prevent you from claiming.

On the other hand, a claim can come to nothing if it can be shown that the claimant voluntarily accepted the inherent risk. For example, a footballer who receives a blow on the leg from another player, by accident, will be met by the defence that it was a sheer accident and that, in any event, the player voluntarily accepted the risk of injury. Such a defence is likely to succeed.

Less widely understood is that a passenger in a vehicle who knows that the driver is drunk, will be faced with an argument that he voluntarily accepted a risk when he accepted the lift. This is unlikely to be a total defence if the driver subsequently crashes the vehicle, but the claimant is likely to have his damages pared back by a percentage for his contributory negligence in voluntarily accepting the risk of the situation.

Timetable of an accident claim
or don't always blame your solicitor!

		Time lapse
Road accident occurs	1 January 1987	
Solicitor consulted by family.	8 January 1987	one week
Solicitor lodges legal aid application.	10 January 1987	
Limited legal aid granted.	12 March 1987	two months
Solicitor asks for medical and police reports, interviews witnesses and may request engineer's report.	22 March 1987	ten days
Medical report received.	1 May 1987	six weeks
Police indicate that the driver you say caused the accident is pleading guilty to driving without due care and attention.	30 June 1987	one month
Police report released.	20 July 1987	three weeks

The papers are ready to go to counsel (a barrister) to draft a statement of claim.	27 July 1987	one week
Counsel returns the papers.	17 August 1987	three weeks
Statement of claim is served on the driver you blame, after your up-to-date losses have been checked.	1 September 1987	two weeks (assuming the client is not on the Costa Brava)
Solicitors for the defendant serve the defence, denying liability. (Technically a defence has to be served within fourteen days, but invariably the time is extended by consent or by court order.)	15 October 1987	six weeks
Discovery and inspection of documents concluded (this period could be less in a straightforward case).	1 December 1987	six weeks

Instructions sent to counsel to advise about legal aid extension.	7 December 1987	one week
Counsel returns papers with advice on merits required by legal aid authority.	4 January 1988	three weeks (even counsel are allowed to celebrate Christmas)
Counsel's opinion sent to The Law Society to authorise extension of legal aid to take case for trial.	5 January 1988	one day
Legal aid authority extend legal aid as requested.	31 January 1988	three weeks
Papers are lodged at Central Office for action to be set down for trial.	14 February 1988	two weeks
Application is made to fix the date for trial in London.	15 March 1988	one month
Date for trial fixed.	15 October 1989	nineteen months

Some/all damages paid over after legal aid clearance.	1 December 1989	six weeks
	Total	thirty-five months

Most of the procedures mentioned above are discussed in detail later, but it is helpful to have an idea at the outset of all the procedures involved and the time it is all likely to take. The timetable above is only a very approximate guide. There are many variables, most of which *add* to the time rather than reduce it.

Other developments, not actually listed above, should also be taking place. These may include further medical examinations by your own specialists and by the specialists retained by the insurers. Your solicitor may well have to visit the site of the accident. If an engineer is involved (because your claim is a difficult one requiring an accident reconstruction) then considerable further time may elapse awaiting his visit and report.

If you are suing two drivers (who blame each other), then extra delay is to be expected. If the driver you are blaming is being prosecuted by the police, but denies any driving offence, then it can sometimes be twelve months before his case is heard. Before then the police will not release their evidence to your solicitor and you may not be able to proceed without that evidence.

In some areas, legal aid applications are taking twelve weeks to process. Some medical consultants take six months to produce a report. Three months is average.

Nine months and more is possible. If the case has to go to court, a delay of six months awaiting trial is certainly average, and longer is by no means unusual.

Your claim cannot be finally disposed of until the medical evidence is clear. It may take the medical consultants three or four years of monitoring progress before they can be sure what the future holds. If so, it is likely that the claim cannot be in court within five years. In the meantime you *may* be entitled to interim damages (see pages 73 and 89) or provisional damages (see page 89).

Even after winning a case, a claimant with legal aid may suffer even more delay in getting the damages into their own pocket. This is usually because of the long-winded arguments which occur over costs, which may have to be 'taxed' (checked) by the court. This universally unpopular procedure has to be concluded before the damages can be released in full. If a large sum of damages has been awarded, then it should be possible to pay a large part over to the claimant *immediately*, the claimant's solicitor retaining sufficient to ensure that the legal aid fund can recover its costs. Until the costs have been met by the losing party, the solicitor must retain, or hand over to the legal aid fund, sufficient damages to safeguard the fund's position. Once the losing party has paid the taxed costs, the final calculations are made, and the damages, or the balance of damages, are handed over.

The
medical
examination

Before which Arthur meets a man in a pub

'What'll you have then, Arthur? Go on . . . have a pint. Cheer yourself up. You've got a face like a wet day in Margate.' Alec Smart, a thirty-three year old car sales-man, with flashy cufflinks, a blue mohair suit and dripping in jewellery, winked at the barmaid. 'Liz. Make it two pints, love. Got to cheer old Arthur up. Since his accident, his leg's so bad that he's not the man he was. Know what I mean—nudge, nudge, wink, wink?'

Arthur grinned wanly. 'You'd be surprised,' he said, rather wishing he hadn't come down to the Feathers for a drink.

'Careful now, Arthur. Careless talk costs claims. You don't want to go round admitting you can . . . do things.' He raised his glass to Arthur. 'Say you can't. Stands to reason. Build up your claim. You know . . . tell the judge. Well . . . tell him you can't walk no more. That you used to jog every week. Played centre forward for Arsenal, taught Ian Botham how to bat. You got me? That's the way to build up your claim.' Alec patted Arthur in a paternal way. 'You're lucky, my son. You can hit the jackpot. Mark my words. Play it up. Make out you can't do your job properly. Get a claim for lost wages. Can't manage the stairs. Difficulty with shoe laces.'

'But it's just not true.' Arthur wiped some froth from his mouth and thought he sounded very old fashioned.

'The truth? What's the truth got to do with it? Come off it, Arthur, this is a war. You've got to con every penny you can out of the insurers.'

Arthur shook his head doubtfully, thinking of the careful advice he'd had from Paul Bright. 'Funny you should be talking about this. I'm having a medical examination tomorrow by some top man in Harley Street. I was just wondering what to tell him.'

'Come on then, my son, you lay it on real thick. No more economy seats on night flights from Luton to Majorca. It'll be first class for you from now on.'

'You mean . . . because there's not enough room in economy for my leg?'

Alec's black moustache twitched as he winked knowingly. 'Always quick to catch on. That's you Arthur. You'll be a millionaire.'

'So what should I say about an old injury? I mean—I fell from a tree and broke the same leg when I was twelve. Now, if I tell this chap in Harley Street, maybe that'll lose me my claim. What do you think?'

Alec Smart put his finger to his lips. 'Forget it. Keep stumm. Nobody else knows about it. And you know me sunshine—I didn't hear nothing. If that comes out, it could ruin everything. Take a lesson from your Uncle Alec. I remember a bloke I met in here. His name was Ted. Now, he had a claim . . .'

Don't listen to smart Alecs like Alec Smart.

Your own solicitor will certainly need a medical report on you so that he can value your claim. Sometimes the insurers are prepared to accept that report when disclosed as being agreed medical evidence. In large claims, or if they are doubtful (perhaps you have a suspicious back injury), the insurers will require their own medical examination. Above all, remember when you are talking to the consultant retained by the insurers that, whilst he *may* be impartial and fair, human nature being what it is, he may well not give you the benefit of the doubt. After all, the insurers are paying him. In medical matters, just as everywhere else, there are grey areas and you should therefore not give the medical consultant for the insurers the chance to be hostile.

The independent consultant instructed by your own solicitor will usually wish to refer to the records and x-rays of the hospital where you were treated following your accident. It is often prudent that he should also see your own GP's notes. However, some GPs record all manner of remarks made by their patients, which my be irrelevant, or downright unhelpful to the claim. When the solicitors for the *insurers* request access to the GP's records, there is no need for the victim to agree to total release. Authority should be given for the release of *relevant* medical records only. The insurers are not entitled to know about other personal and irrelevant matters. It is for the GP then to decide which of his records should be released and, if in doubt, he should consult his patient's solicitor and/or his own professional body such as the Medical Defence Union.

Now for the really smart advice about medical examinations:

- DO tell your solicitor your full medical history before the examination, concealing nothing which may be relevant.

- DO organise your thoughts before seeing the medical consultant, so that you can remember to describe all the *genuine* complaints which you have.

- DO write down a list of the most fundamental complaints if you are worried about forgetting something. You should not, however, produce a list of complaints as long as Gavin Campbell's arm and expect the consultant to read it—he or she may infer that you are obsessed with your case!

- DO remember that your (competent) solicitor will have told the consultant the background to your claim beforehand.

- DO sound enthusiastic about getting better.

- DO describe the accident to the consultant in the same way that you have described it to your solicitor. Consistency matters, and if the consultant you are seeing is retained by the insurers, then remember that you are, in effect, talking to the opposition, and what you say may be used in evidence against you. Pick your words carefully. Careless talk does cost claims. If the other driver struck you when he was going 60 miles per hour, do not exaggerate it to 95 miles per hour to make it sound worse. Your sins will find you out!

- DO remember that consultants deal with injuries like yours every day. They know what problems you should be having from that type of injury. If you invent things, then they will try to catch you out or cast doubt on what you were saying.

- DO remember that consultants set traps during examinations if they are suspicious about what you are saying. They can and do catch out the 'smart Alecs'. Many consultants have watched you enter their premises or will watch you leave to see how you cope with doors, stairs, crutches, getting into cars and the like. They compare that with what you have told them. The differences are sometimes remarkable! Some doctors watch you put your clothes on and off. The claimant who has just said that he cannot do up his shoe laces ruins everything by proceeding to do just that at the close of the examination!

- DO remember that your GP's records and any old hospital records are available. Do not be tempted to conceal old injuries. A good solicitor will know how to deal with the relevance of that injury by working in conjunction with the chosen consultant. It is far better that you volunteer the truth than risk being exposed as a cheat.

- DO remember that if the case ends up in court, you, the victim, start a goal up by having the sympathy of the judge. You should not risk losing that advantage by exaggerating your medical problems, either at the trial itself, or at the medical examinations which go before.

- DO remember that judges prefer medical reports which comment that you have made light of your injuries and that you are working hard to get better. It will go against you if a consultant reports that 'there is no obvious explanation for the complaints' or (worse still) that 'it is thought the patient's complaints will diminish once the litigation has been concluded', or (worst of all) that 'the patient is a malingerer'. These are the factors which count when the judge comes to evaluating your claim. Can he trust what you are saying? Have you been caught out in an unguarded moment?

- DON'T score own goals by lying or deliberate exaggeration.

- DON'T volunteer all the details of the evidence about your accident to the medical consultants because, if they record it, it may become part of the evidence in the case and you may be helping the opposition in ways which they could not have dared to hope. Worse still, consultants may paraphrase what you have said *inaccurately* because such details are less important to them. They are interested in the broad picture of what happened to you as a matter of background. The least said about how the accident occurred the better.

- DON'T underestimate the power of insurers to expose you if they're suspicious. It is entirely ethical for them to hire enquiry agents who will follow you, film you or make enquiries in places where you may be known. A bill of £500 would be money well spent if is showed that you were a cheat and a liar. It could save the insurers thousands—at *your* expense!

As a final warning, there is at least one medical consultant (frequently retained by insurers) who traps the unwary by using two recording systems during the examination. It is perfectly proper for a consultant to explain that he or she is going to tape record the answers you give, to help prepare the report after the examination, but it is not proper for a *second* recording to be made *secretly*. You may be lulled into thinking you can talk freely because the tape recorder is switched off, but the second machine is in fact secretly running all the time. However improper this may be, this particular consultant obtains remarkable information for insurers. While you should not challenge a consultant on this point (because most, quite rightly, would be outraged), the lesson is to pick your words carefully, to tell the truth and not to volunteer confidential information which the consultant does not need to know for the purpose of the medical examination. If the consultant is secretly double-recording, nothing will be gained if you have nothing to hide.

The insurers make their first move

In which Arthur hears something to his advantage

There was still a nasty aching around Arthur's knee joint and with his shortened leg he walked with a curious rolling gait, even more so now that the surgeon had fixed his ankle-joint with a pin in a procedure called arthrodesis. But he could walk without crutches and the plaster had long gone. Stairs were still a problem, a fact of which he was painfully aware as he climbed up to the offices of Bright and Keen. He was feeling miserable and his face, which rarely radiated joy anyway, was as long as a dachshund.

As he entered reception, he met Paul Bright, who was selecting a hefty tome from the shelves. 'Ah! Morning, Arthur.' It was the first time he'd called the client by his first name, but it seemed a natural development, though Arthur was far from feeling ready to call his solicitor Paul. 'Let's go straight in, shall we?'

Arthur followed, struggling to keep pace along the corridor with the keen-stepping young lawyer. 'You're walking better,' said Paul Bright as he stopped, turned and watched his client's progress over the last few yards. 'Bit of a gait. Like an old sailor rolling home, clutching a bottle of rum.'

'No rum, but I did have a boat out on the Serpentine once,' Arthur chuckled as he settled into the black moquette chair, whilst the solicitor opened the files on his desk and spread out the papers in front of him.

'Before I tell you what's been happening here, how have you been getting on?'

Arthur wasn't sure what to say. 'Come along pretty well really. I'm doing a full day's work but there are rumblings there. Still no cricket and just when England need me. Did you hear the lunchtime score? 47 for 6. Send for Arthur, that's what I say. Even with my bad leg, I must be better than some of them.' His face sagged again. 'No, seriously, I've been feeling a bit down and it's just been one thing after another at home.'

'I'm sorry to hear that. What's the trouble?'

'Firstly I'm worried about my wife, Jackie. She's got this bee in her bonnet that she needs cosmetic surgery. She's going into some wretched clinic for a facelift. I've told her she doesn't need one, that if anyone needs one it's me. She saw this place advertised and reckons it'll take fifteen years off her. I said, why should I care?' He played with the button on the cuff of his jacket. 'It'll just make me seem like her father.'

Paul Bright shared his concern. 'I hope this is being done by a proper surgeon. Things go wrong with some of these cowboys. Was it arranged through your doctor?'

'No. That's what worries me.' Arthur shook his head dolefully.

Paul Bright debated with himself what to say. 'Oh, I suppose it'll be all right, but she really should see her GP. If it does go wrong then, not only has she got to live with it, but medical negligence claims are rather difficult.'

'I'll tell her, but she won't listen, I'm sure. Then I've got trouble with Wayne, he's my eldest and, to top it all, my mother is driving me mad. She had a fall in a supermarket, broke her arm and settled her own claim for £750. Said she knew better than to see one of your lot—as she put it. Mind you, she took her revenge on the supermarket manager with her umbrella. Caught him a right wallop apparently. Just below the ear!'

'With her good arm, no doubt. Quite a woman, but rather daft to settle a compensation claim without advice.' He stopped to pull a letter from his file. 'Well, do you want the good news or the bad news?'

'Give me the good.'

'The insurers have made an offer.'

'And the bad?'

'It's far too little. So the bad news isn't really bad at all. It's the first step. The day insurers come forward with their best offer first time round, I shall do an Irish jig in the middle of the High Street. It's that unlikely.'

'So tell me what's been going on.'

'Armed with the police report and Hacking-Gore's views, I applied for an interim payment—that's a payment on account of the final value of your claim. Obviously, until he can be more certain about the future, there's no way I'm going to settle finally. I swore a statement, called an affidavit, stating that you had a pretty good chance of succeeding if the claim went to court. I relied on the police report, then added the medical evidence and finally flung in the details of your out-of-pocket expenses. The summons is due to be heard in three weeks.'

'So why the offer?'

'Good question. Two reasons. Firstly, they're trying to put off the risk of the Master, who's a type of judge, awarding a larger sum than they really want to pay as an interim payment, and secondly, they are trying to smoke out from me what I think the final claim is worth.'

Arthur could contain himself no longer. 'So what have they offered?'

'£3,500. It's piffling.' Paul Bright made a chopping motion through the air, as if decapitating the chairman of the insurance company. 'I've told them I'll put an interim offer of £8,500 to you. No Master is going to give you the full value of your claim. They have to err on the cautious side and must be pretty positive that you're going to win because otherwise, if you got a big cheque, spent it and then lost the case, the insurers would have a devil of a job getting their money back from you.'

'So we're going to court. To this Master. Do I have to appear?'

'You'll be glad to hear you don't. If it goes that far, then it'll be argued between solicitors. My guess is that I'll get another phone call from the other side, offering a deal. In fact, if they're cheeky, they might even make an offer to settle conclusively, tempting you not to wait for the final medical evidence.'

'And if they do that?'

'I wouldn't let you settle—at least not without you understanding what you were doing. It's most unwise to settle too quickly. And that's not because I'm too greedy to wait for my fees. It's because it's in your interests to fight on.'

'I'll do what you say. But tell me . . . how can you be confident about the value of the case? We were going to discuss that, weren't we?'

'I'll keep it very simple. The first part of your claim is what we boring old lawyers call 'general damages'. In America, lawyers sue for a particular sum for personal injuries, talking freely of figures with lots of noughts on the end. Over here, it is very unusual to suggest to the judge a particular amount for general damages. It's all rather coy—one of those daft traditions, along with the other charade that it should never be mentioned that the defendant has the benefit of insurance cover. What you'd think would be sensible at the trial of the case is for our side to say that your claim is worth £75,000 and for the other side to say that it's worth £60,000 and for the judge to make up his mind—or *her* mind, I should say! But we can't do that. We can only point the judge in the right way and hope that when his feet do touch the ground, he moves them our way. If the judge is feeling bullish, then you might get £80,000 and if he's bearish, it might be £60,000. Against the US, our system of determining damages is like comparing Noddy's playground with Las Vegas! Even in Scotland, it's a bit different. There the claim is not for damages, but for 'solatium'. The claim *is* for a specific sum of money, and the judge cannot award more than the amount claimed—although he can award less!'

'So what do general damages cover?'

'The pain and suffering, the hassle of the plaster, the hospitalisation, the crutches, the loss of the chance to live a normal way of life while you are recovering. Those are the immediate basics. Then they cover things you can no longer do, such as your cricket. Then they take into account the medical problems which may lie ahead of you. In your case, you've got your fixed ankle joint, the leg shortening and there's going to be some nasty arthritis problems round your kneecap. If the medical evidence is correct, then in fifteen years time you're going to have a lot of trouble. Either you're going to be even more crippled, or you're going to have a new kneecap. Kneecap replacement at the moment isn't very effective. Hopefully, in fifteen years time, it will be. Otherwise you're going to have problems in getting about.'

'So those are all the factors for general damages, are they?'

'Not quite. There's a sub-division called 'handicap on the labour market'. This means that, even if you're in a job now, we have to consider whether, if you were ever to lose that job, you would be in real difficulties in getting employment again because of your injuries. Now, happily in your case, whilst your leg injuries are serious, so far you've been able to hold down your job, but if you were to lose it, then you're less likely to land another one than a fit person. In those circumstances, the judges assess your chances of being out of work and having difficulty in getting another job. They are not very generous and often the award is only about £2,500. If the risk is low, it drops as low as £500 and it's quite difficult to push it up as far as £5,000.'

Arthur nodded thoughtfully. 'So how *do* you work out what the other part of my claim is worth. The general damages to which I *am* entitled?'

'It's basically through experience. That's one of the reasons why you need a specialist solicitor.'

'Just as well I'm not over at the Ponderosa then,' said Arthur emphatically, nodding his head in the direction of Mr Ponder's office. 'What's my claim worth then?

'With the medical uncertainty I can't say finally but, from what I know at the moment, the general damages are going to be at least £15,000. On top of that, there's the labour market handicap, and we've yet to consider future loss of earnings. When you last came in, you felt that your job was secure and you weren't losing any money. Now I gather you are less certain?'

Arthur looked doubtful. 'There's a nasty whiff of redundancy in the air. Not just me. Quite a lot of people. My employers have been taken over by an American outfit and it looks a bit like survival of the fittest. As you know, my job as warehouse manager is basically pen-pushing, but it does involve a fair amount of time going up and down stairs, organizing deliveries, stacking and collection. It's quite high pressure and these Americans aren't concerned about English redundancy laws and 'first in—last out' when choosing people for redundancy. They'll just pay me the compensation and give me the bullet if it suits them, and my guess is it's coming any time.'

Paul Bright's eyes told of his sympathy for his client. 'That's bad but better to know that now rather than later—after your claim has been finalised. If the axe falls, then what we have to prove is that, but for your accident, you wouldn't have been selected for the chop. I'd then do some complex calculations about future wage losses which are part of the general damages, though they don't carry interest.'

Arthur felt confused on hearing that. There was a pause whilst he debated whether to ask something. 'Look Mr Bright, I don't know how to put this, but a chap in the pub was telling me there was no interest on the damages and that all this delay was costing me! I thought you told me I get interest at least?'

Mock irritation flickered across Paul Bright's face, but then he laughed heavily, throwing back his head, 'Look,' he said kindly, 'the sooner you stop listening to pub talk the better. Don't give a Four X for advice from E. Worthington. The rules on interest are complex. On pain and suffering damages you get 2% interest from when the writ is served. On this, you do better in Scotland—there the courts have more discretion and are usually much more generous. On special damages, covering out-of-pocket expenses, it's much the same in England and Scotland—you normally get interest at half the judgment debt rate from the date of accident to trial, which means you'll be getting about 5 or 6%. It varies with interest rates generally. You don't get interest on future loss of earnings or for handicap on the labour market.'

'2%! I can get better than that from my building society.'

'You're right. The law here's in a bit of a mess. The

theory is that your damages are going up with inflation so that, if they give you a true rate of interest on top, you'd be over-compensated.'

Arthur felt rather sheepish as he rose to leave, wishing he hadn't listened to Alec Smart. 'It's funny how people in pubs always seem to know everything and are so dogmatic.'

'Well it's free advice. You take it for what it's worth . . . but it could be a *bitter* experience.' They both groaned, as Paul Bright shook hands and ushered his client to the door. He watched Arthur go down the corridor. The gait was slightly more pronounced now, just as it should be after being seated for three quarters of an hour. There was no doubt about it, poor old Arthur was suffering.

Interim payments

To qualify for an interim payment, the vital ingredients are:

- You must have a substantial claim and a substantial chance of winning it. You must be able to show this in writing, as no oral evidence is allowed.

- The person from whom you are claiming compensation must be insured or must be a substantial person or body, or a public authority.

- You must have medical evidence to support your claim.

- If you wish to claim for your out-of-pocket expenses (known as special damages) you must have available the documents in support.

Be your own best friend

Here are some more do's and don'ts. These are designed to help your solicitor formulate your damages claim in the best possible way, and to preserve the sanity of both of you while the case progresses:

- DO tell your solicitor *everything* and not just what *you* think he or she should hear. Your solicitor must know the full story, warts and all. The good points may not be as good as you think and the bad ones may not be as bad or, if they are, then a well chosen solicitor will know how to deal with them.

- DO give your full medical history.

- DO keep details and documents relating to out-of-pocket expenses.

  These specific items of loss are called special damages. The cost of repairing a watch, the cost of replacing damaged clothing, actual loss of earnings, the cost of travelling to hospital and the cost of medicine are all typical examples. If an item of special damages (such as loss of earnings or the cost of long term medicines) will continue after the trial date or a negotiated settlement, then the loss is no longer called 'special damages' but forms part of the future losses which are assessed under the broad heading of general damages.

- DO claim all State Benefits to which you are entitled (see page 37).

- DO understand that measuring general damages is a job for an expert. Your own leg injury, back injury or whatever, may be identical to someone else's but it is the effect upon *you* that counts. If you were to lose an eye, the effect would be serious. If you are an airline pilot and you lose an eye, the result would be very serious. If you only had one eye before the accident, then the loss of that good eye would be catastrophic. The measure of damages in each case would be totally different.

- DON'T become a 'Mr Allbran', who rings his solicitor as regular as clockwork, every day, asking for an update. Obviously, if there seems to be no progress and it is inexplicable, you must ask—but your chosen solicitor, if any good, should have the matter well under control anyway and should be keeping you informed of everything relevant.

● DON'T expect miracles. There is no reason why your case should reach a conclusion any more quickly than anyone else's. When you were a child, Christmas came no sooner by thinking about it all the time. So, with litigation, it is best not to let it dwell on your mind. Sometimes this actually prevents you getting better. To understand why things take so long, look again at the timetable of events on page 51.

● DON'T be misled by newspaper reports of other cases where it seems that someone in your position got much more than you think you are going to get. Remember:

— the newspaper report may be inaccurate or sensationalised.

— your solicitor has access to thousands of awards which have been properly recorded, and knows how to compare your case with them, when all the facts are known. If the case is complex, you will also have the help of counsel (a barrister in England; an advocate in Scotland).

— the newspaper report may not differentiate between any number of ingredients, so that a headline telling of an award of £250,000 for someone with a leg injury could be very misleading. Here are just some of the ingredients which may well have gone into that award:

damages for pain and suffering; damages for loss of amenity; damages for hiring a home help; damages for hiring a gardener; damages for the continuing cost of medical treatment; damages for attendance of a nurse from time to time; damages for the cost of further operative treatment; out of pocket expenses; actual loss of earnings; future loss of earnings; damages for handicap on the labour market; cost of adaptation of property (or, in extreme cases, some costs of acquisition of property); cost of adaptation of car (or, in extreme cases, cost of acquisition of car); cost of medical aids, such as spare wheelchair; cost of mobile telephone; interest.

See also page 130, when Paul Bright eventually values Arthur's claim, and 'the million pound claim' on page 128. Meanwhile, here are some examples of typical awards:

- loss of an eye £17,500

- tetraplegia .... £85,000+

- severe brain damage with insight
  into condition .... £65,000+

- minor whiplash injury £1,500

- serious whiplash injury £8,500

- serious lung damage (eg asbestosis) £25,000

- minor back strain £1,000

- serious back injury requiring spinal fusion £10,000+

The wide variation in damages for broken legs and arms makes general advice somewhat meaningless. The measure of damages will depend on the nature of the fracture and the particular effect of that fracture upon the claimant. A broken leg could therefore have vastly different values, say £1,500 to £20,000 or more.

Loss
of
earnings
claims

In which Arthur gets an Irishman's rise

Arthur stepped out of the lift on the third floor with feelings of some trepidation. No one, but no one, ever went to the third floor, except by invitation. Thrusting Enterprises plc, who had employed Arthur for the last twenty-three years, had their headquarters in a modern block, looking out towards Crystal Palace. Arthur, as warehouse manager, had an office on the ground floor. Only the chairman and directors, together with their personally invited visitors, walked, as Arthur was now doing, along the thickly carpeted corridor leading to the managing director's office. Thomas Thrusting, son of the founder of the company and known to everybody as TT, had recently sold out to the Americans. Now the watchful eye of Wall Street was on him and change was in the air. There had been a number of redundancies.

Timidly Arthur knocked on the door. 'Come,' the voice of TT boomed and Arthur was then in the presence, standing in front of a huge desk, behind which sat TT himself, resplendent in Savile Row suit and Jermyn Street shirt. 'Good morning Arthur. How nice of you to call in. Please sit down.'

Arthur did so, perching uncomfortably on the edge of the wicker-bottomed chair. 'Good morning TT,' he croaked in a voice dry with apprehension.

'Now look Arthur, I'll come straight to the point. Everyone holds you in the highest possible esteem and regard. Your dedication to the company is second to none and the levels of efficiency you have brought to the warehouse will always be an example of what can be done.' TT's head nodded thoughtfully, his blue eyes radiating sincerity. Arthur was pleasantly surprised, having expected that he was to be made redundant.

'Thank you TT. It's most kind of you to say so.'

'Not at all, not at all. But your injuries have hit you hard. It's because we think so much of you that

79

I've made a special recommendation to the board, who have, I'm delighted to say, accepted my suggestion. As from now we are giving you a new and challenging opportunity with a dual function. Firstly, you'll be in charge of the purchase of all carbon paper.' Here TT paused to make it sound as if Arthur would have a multi-million pound budget. 'Secondly, and most importantly, you will maintain a watching brief over the entire warehouse. Now that we have our new American computer, you need not involve yourself in the day to day trivia of running the warehouse. You will, however, report to me on a one to one basis.' TT paused and fixed Arthur with a knowing look. 'I can see you are impressed. But don't thank me. You deserve it. We've created an opportunity for you, a springboard to further greatness.'

Arthur beamed across the wide open desk top. 'Thank you TT.' He wanted to ask about the pay rise but felt that would be churlish. However, as if he'd read Arthur's mind, TT opened Arthur's personnel file and glanced at a letter which he then pushed across the desk.

'You will understand Arthur that we couldn't give you this golden opportunity and still maintain you at the same income. You wouldn't have expected that, would you Arthur?' The steely blue eyes fixed Arthur once again, who nodded his head vigorously in agreement, wondering just how big the rise would be. 'Of course, I knew you would understand that. Now, at the present time, your income is £12,000 a year. As from now, you will have a salary of £9,000, but of course, the incremental scale . . . well Arthur, I can only say that the sky's the limit. As your learning curve develops, I can see that you'll be pushing for promotion—maybe up to board level before many years are out and then . . . who knows? Perhaps an income of £20,000 per year and a company car.' TT raised both hands in mock protest. 'No, don't thank me Arthur. You've *earned* this opportunity. Now just go out and prove me right. And thank you for dropping by.'

Arthur stood up, head spinning at all this talk of learning curves and incremental opportunities. A place on the board! And reporting personally to TT. 'I'm most grateful to you TT. Thank you TT.'

But for his fixed ankle joint and uncertain kneecap, Arthur would have strutted like a peacock down the corridor as he returned to the lift. Now he'd be visiting the third floor again. And again. Reporting personally to TT. He went down to the cubby hole by the warehouse which was his office, only to find that, in the few brief minutes whilst he had been upstairs, the carpet had been removed. There was a knock on the door. It was Harry, the company carpenter. 'Morning, Arthur. Shan't be a moment. Just taking your name off the door. Only departmental heads have that privilege, as you know.'

'Yes,' replied Arthur uncertainly. 'But I've got special responsibilities now. Highly confidential of course.' Suddenly he wasn't sure. A pay cut of £3,000 a year? That was a bit harsh for the chance of doing two jobs and all the learning curves and company cars in the future. He was even less happy when Florrie, the tea lady, dropped by and said that he'd have to collect his own tea in future. Only departmental heads had tea delivered to them.

He decided to ring Paul Bright.

'So,' said Paul Bright, 'you've had an Irishman's rise.'

'You mean, I've been demoted?' Arthur looked crestfallen.

'That's right. TT dressed it up well. He was not seeking to make you redundant. He was not saying outright that you were being demoted because of your accident. He was changing your entire job description, cutting your salary by £3,000 a year. Obviously I don't know how he sees it but you tell me that you've been coping well with the job.'

'So what do I do?' Arthur was thoroughly confused and feeling very depressed, as the implications of the meeting with TT sank home.

'Let's run through the possibilities,' said Paul Bright. 'Firstly, you could walk out of the job and go to the Industrial Tribunal. You would argue that de-motion is a constructive dismissal and that you don't want your new role at £3,000 per year less. That may lead the company to do two things. TT would either argue that because of your injuries, you were no longer up to your job and that he was merely being kind by finding a niche for you. Alternatively he would declare you redundant. If he did this, then you would get your redundancy payment but you would scarcely be a rich man on that. If the Tribunal decided that the company was right and that you were no longer up to your previous job, then you would not succeed in a claim for constructive dismissal either.'

'So what do I do?'

'The plain fact is that, at the age of forty-three, with a very serious leg injury, getting another job is not going to be easy. You might find yourself job hunting for years. If you can bear to carry on working for TT after this, then I suggest that I visit him to obtain a statement confirming that he has taken this decision solely because of your injuries. I'm sure this is true. If he can see the wisdom in co-operating then you will have a job *and* you will have a claim for the loss in earnings at the rate of £3,000 per year, less tax.'

'And if I can't bear to work there?'

'You claim for constructive dismissal in the Industrial Tribunal. If the company argues the redundancy point and succeeds, then you get your redundancy payment but you have no job. Worse still, you would have to prove that your loss of earnings after that stemmed from the injuries, *not* from company recession. That seems to me to be unpalatable. It would be better if the company ran the argument before a Tribunal that you had been demoted because of your injuries. If the company succeeds on that, then you get no compensation for constructive dismissal in the Industrial Tribunal, but you do have a very large claim for future loss of earnings in your damages suit. On the other hand, you have no job. You have a wife and three children. In your position I suggest that you stay in the job so as long as TT gives me a suitable statement which supports a claim for the drop in earnings, which I shall then claim against the other car driver.'

'Suppose I take your advice and accept this pay cut. You claim £3,000, less tax, against the other driver. How long does that go on? Till I'm sixty-five when I would normally retire?'

'No. The loss of earnings from the date of demotion to the date of trial is calculated mathematically and you get the precise sum. For loss of earnings in future years, the courts apply a multiplier based on your age. You're forty-three now, with twenty-two working years ahead of you, barring calamities. Let's assume that your loss of earnings, after tax, is £2,000 a year. The court will not multiply £2,000 by twenty-two years because of all the uncertainties in the future anyway. The judge will probably multiply the £2,000 by a factor of eight to ten years.'

'And suppose after the trial I change jobs and get another one at £12,000 a year?'

Paul Bright grinned. 'I wondered whether that thought might have occurred to you. If, after the trial, you have a lucky break and get a better job and you are no longer suffering a loss of earnings, then you keep the damages. It would be different if you had deliberately misled the court about the position.'

'Just so that I get everything clear in my mind,' said Arthur, 'if I walk out of this job, saying that I can't stand the insult, then, if I can prove that this situation arose because of my injuries, I get a total loss of earnings claim, based on £12,000 per year after tax. Is that right?'

'Exactly. But of course you have to try and find a job at the best possible salary to *mitigate* your loss. If at the trial the judge was satisfied that you were unemployable, then he would calculate the loss of earnings to the trial and for the future would apply the multiplier of eight or ten. If he decided on the evidence that you would get a job after two years at the same income, then the award into the future would be only for that period. There are so many imponderables.'

Arthur gazed round the room at nothing in particular, as he tried to gather his thoughts. From the next room came the sound of a busy photocopier. Paul Bright realised the difficulty in the decision and sat silently. 'I'll take your advice. I can't afford to walk out of the job. You get a statement from TT which supports a claim against the other car driver for my loss of earnings and I'll stay. If you can't get that statement then I'll have to reconsider.'

'I'm sure that's the best thing to do. And you do realise that these damages for future losses are in addition to your other damages for the injury?'

Arthur stood up. 'Oh yes. I remember what you told me before. It's safer to have a job even without the carpet and having to get my own tea.' Arthur looked thoughtful. 'An Irishman's rise, you called it?' he mused. 'I never knew it was called that. You learn something every day.'

Paul Bright pushed back his chair and stood up. 'Well, in the words of TT—that's all part of the learning curve. Just as he promised you. By the way, how did your wife's cosmetic surgery go?'

'Too soon to say yet but, between you and me, I'd say she looks fifteen years *older*, but maybe it'll settle down. One eye appears to be higher and there's flabby skin round her cheeks. But I can't tell her that.'

Working it out

Loss of earnings arising from an accident are calculated to the date of trial and are part of the 'special damages'.

If you have your own insurance policy against accidents that policy will pay you a sum of money during your absence from work. You are still entitled to claim damages for loss of earnings in addition if your employers did not pay you during your absence.

Many contracts of employment have a term that the employer will advance wages, *as a loan*, whilst you are off work following an accident, to be repaid if a successful claim is made. So long as such an agreement was made before the accident, or (if you are lucky) immediately following an accident and before any payments are made, your claim can include loss of earnings. You must then reimburse your employer when you receive your compensation.

When calculating what wages have been lost after an accident, the following factors are brought into account. The first two are added to the basic amount you claim:

- loss of promotion and pay rise(s) (if provable);

- loss of chance to improve pension.

The next three are deducted:

- tax which would have been paid, had earnings not been adversely affected by the accident;

86

- National Insurance contributions which would have been paid;

- any tax refund made by the Revenue because earnings in the tax year of the accident were not as great as had been expected;

Finally:

- Unemployment Benefit is deducted in full;

- Supplementary Benefit/Income Support is deducted in full;

- Sickness Benefits and Industrial Injury Benefits are deducted in part.

Interim
payments
(again)
and
provisional
damages

In which Arthur collects a cheque

Paul Bright's secretary left the room, leaving behind two cups of steaming coffee and a waft of Givenchy. 'Well Arthur, I've got an excellent statement from TT. He's confirmed that but for your accident, you wouldn't have been demoted. Armed with that I was able to swear another affidavit in support of your application for an interim payment, highlighting the loss of earnings. This really wrong-footed the solicitors for the insurers. At the end of last week I went up to the law courts in the Strand and had the Master in the palm of my hand.'

'So what did I get?'

'£12,500, and the cheque came in this morning's post.'

'Thank you. But doesn't this upset my legal aid?'

'No, interim payments don't count. Otherwise nobody on legal aid would ever apply for an interim payment. Anyway, the other solicitor has now started to sound me out about a final settlement, so I shadow-boxed about a claim for provisional damages. The insurers were warned of this possibility in the statement of claim.'

'Remind me,' said Arthur whilst sipping his coffee. 'Wasn't provisional damages something to do with having two bites at the cherry?'

'That's right. Until quite recently, once you had settled your claim or had it dealt with in court, there was no going back for more compensation if your medical position deteriorated. Now, where the medical evidence suggests that you may suffer deterioration in, say, fifteen years, you can ask the judge to make your award for damages on the most optimistic medical forecast, but reserving the right to claim more within a given period of years, which could be fifteen (or even life), if the worst medical fears materialize.'

'So you mean I have a choice of lower damages now but keeping my rights open or . . .'

'I winkle out of the insurers a deal which finalises the litigation once and for all, taking into account the risk of the worst fears materializing.' Bright cocked his head on one side. 'Most insurers would rather see claims settled once and for all. They don't want the threat of further litigation, further legal costs and uncertain claim values hanging over them. It's untidy. Who knows what the measure of damages will be in fifteen years time? That's why it's worth mentioning provisional damages to them. They are more likely to come forward with a generous offer for a *final* settlement now.'

'Unless you advise me differently, I'd rather have the best possible sum now.'

'Most people say that and, in general, I don't dissuade them. In some cases, where the measure of damages would be dramatically different if the worst materialized, then I would certainly go for provisional damages.' Bright glanced at his client, took in the slightly hunched frame, saw the furrows which had not been there twelve months before. 'Don't rush your decision. Think it over. I'm not advising you to rush into a settlement. The tactic is to leave it to the insurers to make an offer. They know that, until they make a sensible proposition, the claim will grind on. Eventually they will make an offer or, more likely, make a payment into court.'

'What is a payment into court?'

'I'll explain that if it happens. It's fairly complex. Nothing to worry about now.'

'So we just wait?'

'That's the score—wait for a judge to be available which is unlikely to be for eighteen months. Only then need we decide finally whether to go for provisional damages or try some other tactic.'

'That's it for today then.' said Arthur. 'But thanks for the cheque anyway. I'll take Jackie to the Chinese to celebrate.'

It must have been two days after the interview that Paul Bright's secretary walked in clutching a parcel. It was a bottle of malt whisky from Arthur. The solicitor was very moved. The generous gesture was a rare occurrence and one which Arthur could ill afford.

Some tactical strokes

The court has no power to make an order for provisional damages unless the uncertainty relates to *medical matters*. Uncertainty about job prospects or similar issues is not sufficient. Furthermore, the court has to put a time limit on the date by which the further application has to be made. In Scotland, too, the judge can set a time limit.

If the medical uncertainty is something which could be resolved by putting off the original trial for only one or two years, then it may be preferable to press for the largest possible measure of interim damages and to put off the actual trial of the action for that one or two year period, so that the claim can be finally settled on the basis of the best possible medical certainties.

If the medical uncertainty cannot be resolved for, say, two or three years *and* there is a dispute about who was to blame for the accident, your solicitor should advise you of the possibility of going for a split trial. Here the judge determines blame for the accident, but all questions of damages are left over. Very often this tactic leads to an agreement about liability, without the matter going to court. Once that issue has been favourably resolved, it is straightforward to obtain an interim payment because the issues of liability are no longer an impediment.

Insurers do not like split trials because two trials mean two lots of legal costs and two lots of preparation for trial. Also, keeping issues of liability and measure of damages alive at the same time gives more room for manoeuvre and flexibility in negotiating a settlement.

The fewer issues there are between the parties, the easier it is for the claimant's solicitor to know whether what is being offered is fair.

Threatening a split trial is often a good tactic in the plaintiff's armoury.

A procedure called 'judgment under Order 14' or 'summary judgment' is useful if the evidence *on paper* about blame for the accident is clear-cut and in your favour. An application is made to the court, supported by a sworn statement. If the court agrees that there is no worthwhile defence to the claim, judgment will be entered on the question of liability for damages to be assessed later. The court may make an award of interim damages. The advantages of getting judgment are:

- at an early stage in the proceedings you know that you have 'won' the question of who was to blame;

- you do not have to attend court to give evidence;

- once again, insurers lose the tactical advantage of being able to reduce and/or blur their offer on damages by arguing that it is uncertain that you would win on the quesion of liability;

- the judgment carries interest;

- the chances of a trial are considerably reduced since there is now only the question of damages to resolve.

A consultation with Queen's Counsel

In which Arthur learns a salutary lesson

It was 4.20 pm. The sky was drizzly and dark and, as usual in the vicinity of the Law Courts, there was an air of depression as litigants, who had started the day full of hope, emerged to lick their wounds. Even those who had succeeded had been through hours of doubt, legal jargon and nail-biting.

With Paul Bright by his side, Arthur crossed on the zebra outside the courts, passed the 'Wig and Pen' and then turned down Middle Temple Lane. As predicted by Paul Bright sixteen months before, the insurers had left it late to make their move and Arthur's case was fixed for trial in a month's time. In thirty-four days to be precise. Arthur had found that he had been counting the days, as the menace of the courtroom had drawn near. Yet, as he walked beside his solicitor, he could see that Paul Bright was still as calm, self-assured and confident as he'd always been.

'Most of these people walking round here are barristers who have just finished arguing cases in the courts. They get out of their wigs and gowns and scurry back to their offices, which they call chambers, to have meetings, which they call conferences or consultations! In Scotland, these lawyers are called advocates. In fact, my great uncle Angus was an advocate. I think I inherited my taste for whisky from him! Anyway, you'll be seeing Mark Keaton, QC. Everyone calls him 'Buster'. He's at the very top of the tree and I expect he'll be a High Court judge in a year or two. With him he'll have the junior counsel who's been responsible for dealing with the paperwork, like the statement of claim and who, you will remember, advised about the evidence to be called. That's Jeremy Sprigg. The three of us work together throughout the trial, but most of the burden of presenting your case rests with Buster. Whatever happens today, and anything may happen with Buster, don't take it personally.'

Arthur nodded doubtfully as he imagined 'Buster' Keaton as an ogre with three heads, all of them covered with horse-hair wigs. 'Fine.'

'He'll give you a rough ride. It's not his job to pat you on the head and say what a good boy you are. It's his job to win, and that means probing the weakest points in your case, questioning you about them, assessing you as a witness and generally making sure that you have your act together by the time the case goes to court. Though he looks ferocious, they say he's quite kind to old ladies and animals. And just remember—he's on your side, not just today, but when we go to court. If he reduces you to a nasty little pool of perspiration, then just think what he's going to do to the other side when we go to court!'

Arthur laughed nervously. 'Thanks for the warning. Will he wear his wig and gown to see me?'

'No. In chambers he'll be in his court suit, looking somewhere between an undertaker's mate and a punter at Royal Ascot. Here we go. Through this door.'

'What are all these names outside? Are they all partners like in your firm?'

'No. Each barrister is self-employed, and they share the expenses but not what they earn.'

Bright turned to Gilbert, the senior clerk to the chambers, who'd just emerged from the clerks' room. Arthur would have liked a better view of this room, which seemed small but was awash with sets of papers, the air full of telephones ringing as the junior clerks fixed last minute arrangements to get counsel into the right courts, in the right places, at the right times for the following morning.

'Mr Keaton's ready to see you now, if you'd like

to follow me.' To Arthur the journey seemed endless, through sets of doors and up winding stone staircases, down book-lined passages with varying shades of gloom and light, until at last Gilbert opened a door and they were in the presence of the Great Man, who stood up to greet them, six inch cigar in hand, the air thick with the heavy smell of Havana.

'Afternoon Paul. And this will be Mr Henderson? I'm pleased to meet you. And I don't think you've met my junior, Mr Jeremy Sprigg.' After much hand-shaking and friendly bonhomie between solicitor and counsel, they were all seated, 'Buster' Keaton sitting at the head of the table, his pepper and salt hair surrounded by a halo of cigar smoke, his whole personage exuding success. 'Now then Mr Henderson,' his voice boomed across the table, 'I've read all the papers. Mr Bright here tells me that the insurers have paid the sum of £65,000 into court. It's not enough. If you take my advice you'll ignore it.' He turned to Paul Bright. 'Just to make sure there are no misunder-standings, I'll explain the position.'

He waited for Paul Bright to nod before he continued. 'There's no certainty in litigation. There are no written guarantees of success. Even the best cases go wrong. Sometimes because you get a miserable judge. Take today for example—I've been up before Mr Justice Pickler. You'd think he was a shareholder in the insurance company. Getting a decent award out of him is almost impossible. So there you have it—you might get the wrong judge. Another problem is how the evidence comes out. Now, your solicitor has done a good job, putting the evidence together. If all these witnesses say the right things, 'coming up to proof' as we call it, then you should do all right. But witnesses are human. They make mistakes. They forget what they want to say. They sometimes change their story. Expert witnesses can be worse . . . sometimes get crucified. So there you have all the imponderables. We don't know what sort of impression you'll make on the judge but I'll come to that in a moment. You with me so far?' He threw out the challenge with a jab of cigar and a dollop of ash fell on the papers in front of him.

'Yes, I understand all that.'

'Good. Now the insurers have paid £65,000 into court. You know it. I know it. But the judge doesn't. If the case isn't settled, the judge, assuming that he finds the other driver to blame, will award damages. If the judge were ready for the funny-farm, he might find that the accident was entirely your fault. If he did, then you'd leave court with not a penny—not one penny.' He emphasized the point loudly. 'However, I don't think you were to blame but were the judge to find you even 25% to blame, then £65,000 looks slightly attractive.' He looked at Jeremy Sprigg. 'I think you agree with me on that point, don't you Jeremy? We should be all right on liability?' He knew the answer, otherwise he'd never have asked the question.

'Oh yes,' said Jeremy Sprigg. 'I've never had any doubts, neither has Paul.'

'Good. Now then, if the judge awarded you £60,000, then the result is disaster. You get the award of £60,000 but the legal costs incurred by both sides, since this £65,000 was paid into court will have to be paid *by you* out of your damages. The legal aid certificate doesn't help.'

Paul Bright intervened. 'Your case is due to last about a day and a half, or maybe two days, and you should reckon that the costs of the trial might total £20,000 for both sides. So, if the judge awarded you only £60,000 and you had to pay the costs since payment in, though you would get your costs until then paid, you'd end up with only around £40,000.'

'Thank you for that Paul,' said Buster. 'We barristers are notoriously bad on estimating the costs of litigation. It's not so much part of our job,' he added by way of explanation to Arthur Henderson. 'Anyway, if the judge awards you more than £65,000, then you've won and you get whatever sum he awards you and the insurers pick up the bill for the costs. So deciding whether to take this money is critical. 'With me so far?'

Arthur nodded yes.

'I think that I can negotiate a better offer at the courtroom door and, if not, I expect to beat that figure anyway. Nevertheless, if you want a quiet life and £65,000 now—accept the offer and don't think there'll be any hard feelings from us. It's your case and we do what you want.'

Arthur shifted uncomfortably on his chair, knocking off the wooden arm which fell with a clatter. 'Sorry about that,' he stammered, wondering why he always had trouble with chairs, as he picked it up and slotted it back into position. Those around him made soothing noises about the wretched thing always falling off. 'I'd be a fool not to take your advice. I'm in no hurry to settle.'

'Fine. Let's go for it and prove to those Micawbers down at the insurance company that they've got it wrong.' Keaton spread out the papers on the desk. 'Now for the basics. You win if the evidence convinces the judge, on the balance of probabilities, that the other side was to blame. A great deal, therefore, turns on your evidence. I shall leave it to Paul Bright to run through the court procedures with you. My job now is to make an assessment of you, as a witness.'

The Great Man fingered his extravagant side-boards, eyes flashing a critical appraisal which forced

Arthur back in his seat. Instinctively he clung to the arms of the chair, his knuckles white against the dark wood as he looked again at the Queen's Counsel and nodded in understanding. 'The first thing, Mr Henderson is that, although I ask you the questions, *you* address your answers to the judge. Keep your voice up and watch his pen. It's no good gabbling or mumbling. What he doesn't write down is quickly forgotten. That's fundamental. Secondly, don't be cocky and don't get angry under cross-examination when questioned by the other side's barrister, who will be trying to provoke you. Think before you answer questions. Thirdly, don't *volunteer* anything which you have not been asked. Listen carefully to the question and give *brief* answers very much to the point. Have I made myself clear?'

Arthur swallowed hard and nodded, wondering what he would feel like in a courtroom if he felt like this now. 'Yes. I think so.'

The Great Man picked up the proof of evidence, carefully drawn by Paul Bright, which set out Arthur Henderson's version of events. 'Right. I'll try you on a few questions. It's agreed by everyone concerned that you had an accident when a car, which you were driving, was in collision with another vehicle which came out of a side turning in defiance of a Give Way sign. What type of car were you driving?'

Arthur beamed. This was easier than he thought. 'A Maestro. Green coloured. I bought it second-hand from a dealer in Weybridge. It was in good order.'

There was a sharpness in the QC's immediate retort. 'Come now Mr Henderson. The answer to that question should have been—"my car was a Maestro." I didn't ask about whether it was new, second-hand or its colour. Don't volunteer. Let's try again. On with the next question. Where were you going in your Maestro?'

'Well, my wife, she wanted some dry cleaning fetched and so I'd just done that and she'd said "mind you don't forget to collect's Grandma's indigestion tablets." She suffers that way. So I was going down to Boots in the High Street.'

'Mr Henderson, you and I will get along very well if you listen to my question and listen to the advice I've given to you.' The voice was ever so slightly raised, the tone ever so slightly tetchy. 'I don't want to know about your Grandma's indigestion. I don't care if she has more wind than the Foden Works Brass Band. It won't help you win your case to tell the judge that. Listen to the question and just answer it.' The Queen's Counsel glanced across at Paul Bright and, when Arthur wasn't looking, raised his eyes to the heavens in despair.

'I'm sorry.' Arthur stretched out his aching leg under the table, catching Jeremy Sprigg rather a nasty blow just above the shin.

'Ouch!' Sprigg exclaimed, uncertain of his assailant. He was rewarded from a withering glare from Buster Keaton, but Arthur said nothing.

'Now let's try again Mr Henderson. 'Were you alone when this accident occurred?'

'No. I mean—yes. I mean, I'd just dropped off my daughter Kate. No. I tell a lie.' He scratched his head in confusion and his face puckered into a gigantic frown. 'It wasn't Kate. It was Susie. She was going to a fancy dress party. I can remember it well. Yes. I'd definitely dropped her off just before the accident occurred. Yes I was alone,' he concluded triumphantly, looking across the table to see the impression which he'd made.

The reaction was immediate. Keaton let the proof

of evidence fall, smacked both his hands palm-down on the table so that the ginger nuts leapt in startled unison, much in time with Arthur Henderson. As Keaton leaned back frowning his disapproval, Arthur realised, just too late, that he'd done it again.

'Yes Mr Henderson. And does your dog have fleas?'

Arthur looked puzzled. 'Dog? I haven't got a dog.'

'Thank you Mr Henderson. That's the first question you've answered without telling me the life history of your car, your family, your grandmother's wind and of all the social functions you've attended since William the Conqueror crossed the Channel.'

The scowl on the Great Man's face as he spoke would be etched on Arthur's mind until his dying day. The eyes had nearly disappeared beneath the bushy eyebrows but could still bore into Arthur's numbed brain. There was an embarrassed silence. Keaton continued, his voice now kind and gentle. 'Mr Henderson, I hope that you've learnt a lesson. It's up to you to sell your case. When you're in that witness box, you're alone. You'll have the sympathy of the court, so long as you don't lose it.' Forgetting that he had no wig on, he clasped both hands on top of his head and pulled his hair forward by mistake, a movement often done by him through habit. 'If that had been your evidence in court, you'd be well on the way to losing. We'll try again. And again.'

For the next half an hour Arthur went through every detail of the accident, his answers getting more concise, more carefully thought out and more punchy until, at last, 'Buster' Keaton expressed satisfaction. 'Good. Now keep it like that if we have to go in to court. I'm still hoping that I'll negotiate a settlement but you can never tell. Do you have any questions?'

Arthur thought for a moment and then replied with a question which had always troubled him. 'What do I call the judge?'

'So long as you show respect, the judges don't mind what they're called. As your case is in the High Court, then you should call the judge "My Lord" or "Your Lordship". I've heard one witness who insisted on saying "Your Majesty". The judge suggested to him that "Your Lordship" would do but the witness would have none of it and replied that "there was no need for the judge to be coy about his proper title".'

Arthur joined in the laughter. The grilling was now over. 'If your case had been in the county court, then you call the judge "Your Honour".' He glanced at his watch. 'I think we've covered everything. Paul, if there's any further approach from the insurers, let me know, but otherwise we shall meet about an hour before the case is due to start. You'll take the other witnesses through their proofs and explain the procedures generally to Mr Henderson here?'

'Yes. Leave all that to me.'

Strategic moves by the other side

Paying money into court is the strongest weapon in the insurers' armoury. It should not be assumed that money paid into court by insurers is a correct valuation of the claim. A clever payment into court is likely to be a sum which is insufficient, temptingly hard to refuse and which, nevertheless, creates a risk that some judges will not award as much.

Occasionally the amount paid in will be derisory, either because the insurers are using it as a shock tactic or because they take the view that the claim is only worth settling on a nuisance value basis.

Listen carefully to your (good) solicitor's advice. Experience will enable him or her to understand the way in which the insurance company are thinking.

If you have legal aid, then your solicitor must tell the legal aid authorities about the offer. If your solicitor believes that the sum should be accepted and you do not agree, then there is a strong chance that you will lose your legal aid, as public funds will not support you if you are being unreasonable in your demands or expectations.

A decision whether the sum is acceptable has to be taken within twenty-one days of money being paid into court. If accepted, then the money is paid out of court to the solicitor for the claimant, who is entitled to have his standard costs paid by the opposition. *After* the twenty-one day period, the offer cannot be accepted without the other side's consent or without the leave of the court.

The insurers are entitled to make more than one payment into court and quite often do, topping up the first offer to add increased pressure as the trial draws near. The last payment in, to be properly effective, must be made twenty-one days before the trial starts.

In Scotland, the tactic of the defender is to place pressure on the claimant (there called the 'pursuer'), not by paying money into court, but by a similar procedure called 'tender'. This is an offer made in writing; the money is not sent to the court, but the consequences are similar to those of payment into court.

At any time in this type of claim, the insurers can make an offer to settle. They may make it in 'Without Prejudice' correspondence or across the table talking to your solicitor. They may make more than one offer and frequently do. Normally, insurers do make informal offers before taking the step of paying money into court. This is because they prefer to sound out what sum a claimant wants, before deciding how much to pay in. Just because the offer is made across the table, or even by telephone rather than by way of payment into court, does *not* mean that the offer is not a fair or generous one. It may be. Every offer has to be carefully considered by your solicitor, but an informal offer, not made by way of payment into court, does not carry the same penalty on costs if rejected as does a payment into court. That is why, almost invariably, insurers do end up making a payment into court some time before the trial.

All
ready
for
the
trial

In which Arthur learns of both trials and
tribulations

'Oh, look,' enthused Arthur to his wife, as he opened his post after getting back from his day's work at Thrusting Enterprises. 'Paul Bright has sent me details of what happens at the hearing of my case. He says that he's been asked for an explanation so often that he's had a special document prepared.'

'Looks a bit complicated. Let's read it over a cup of tea.'

'Are you sure you want to go through all that, Arthur?' asked Jackie dubiously, glancing quickly through all the pages. She always kept her eyes lowered these days, since her cosmetic surgery.

'I don't *want* to, but I'd be throwing money away if I accepted the offer. Anyway, all that procedure is nothing for me to worry about. That's their job. Funny, isn't it, just how much they have to know, how much they have to do to get a case like this put together properly.'

'Just as well old Ponder isn't acting for you. That would be a disaster.' Jackie poured another cup of tea and gave Arthur a slice of one of Mr Kipling's 'exceedingly good' cakes. 'There's something I've been meaning to tell you.' She looked rather apologetic.

'Oh yes? You mean about your cosmetic surgery?'

Jackie shook her head. 'No. I'm consulting Paul Bright about that as soon as your case is out of the way. That's if he wins.'

'No, dear. That's the wrong approach. You shouldn't consult him only if I win. You consult him because he's the right person for the job. You should go to him, even if I lose.'

Jackie thought about it for a moment. 'You're right. But anyway I wasn't going to talk about that. It's about Wayne. You know he had that accident at work, when he got caught up in that machine?'

Arthur grimaced at the mention of his trouble-some son. 'Awkward so-and-so but he didn't deserve that to happen to him.'

'Well, as you know, he wasn't in the union and he's decided to make a claim.'

Arthur stirred his tea, his brow furrowed. 'After all this time? He'd better see Paul Bright straightaway. But you know he never listens to me. You tell him.'

'That's just the point. He'd gone to see old *Ponder*. I'm sure he does it just to spite you. He knows what you think of Will Ponder. This is just Wayne's way of expressing himself.'

'He's always expressing himself in his own way. It's no good me telling him to see Paul Bright. If you can't persuade him, he'll have to take his chance down at the Ponderosa . . .' Arthur shrugged. 'Anyway, love, I'm far more worried about you. Let's get my claim out of the way, then we can decide what we do about your cosmetic surgery problem.'

Jackie glowered angrily. 'Go on. Admit it. That so-called plastic surgeon shouldn't be allowed to fillet haddock, let alone hack about people's faces. Tell me the truth. I look dreadful now, don't I?'

Arthur wanted to be kind, yet truthful. 'Well, I wouldn't exactly say that. I'm getting used to it. But it certainly wasn't the success it should have been.' He was keen to change the subject. 'Anyway, my case will all be over within two days—tomorrow if it settles. I've got to be at the law courts in the Strand at 9.30. I must read through my proof of evidence. That's what Paul Bright told me to do.'

He shifted uncomfortably on his faded moquette chair. 'I'll tell you what, love. If I win, the first thing I'm going to do is to buy a new chair. We bought this when we were married. It's so uncomfortable anyone would think a herd of elephants had been tap dancing on the springs.'

Jackie shook her head. 'Nothing like that. It's only used by you and Gran.'

Arthur rose from the chair and peered at it suspiciously. 'That explains everything. I'd forgotten she's taken to using it when I'm not here.' He pushed it, prodded it and probed until, with a shout of triumph, he found what he had been looking for. With a flourish he produced Gran's missing knitting needle. 'Gran'll be the death of me one day. Where is she anyway?'

'There's no need to be like that Arthur. I know you're het up about your court case. Gran's down at the bookies. You know she always goes there on Tuesdays.'

A document for clients of Bright & Keen explaining what happens at a trial and why it is not quite the same as on TV

Here is the paper which Paul Bright gave to Arthur. It describes what happens at the trial of an accident compensation case, which is a civil case, and quite unlike most trials seen on TV.

People seeking compensation for accident or injury usually proceed in the county court if the claim is below £5,000 or in the High Court if it is above this figure. In either court the procedure is fairly similar. Most cases with serious personal injury are heard in the High Court, the most complex and important cases being dealt with by a High Court judge. Some cases in the High Court are now transferred to the county court against the wish of the parties.

In Scotland, major claims are commenced in the Court of Session, and lesser claims in the Sheriff Court.

What follows is the normal order of events at the trial.

The opening: Counsel for the plaintiff (or pursuer, in Scotland)—the person claiming compensation— outlines the facts and relevant documentation to the judge. There is no jury. The judge decides everything, and will have read the 'pleadings', which are the documents setting out the basis of the claim and reasons why the defendant, ie the opponent, resists payment.

If the medical reports have been agreed, these will also have been lodged with the court in advance, so that the judge will have read them. If the medical evidence has not been agreed because the medical consultants for each side have differed in their conclusions, then the judge will not have seen the medical evidence, but will know from the statement of claim the nature of the injuries. In the opening address counsel will merely highlight the present position and the effect the injuries have had.

The judge will be told of any agreements about particular items of damage, such as travelling expenses. The judge may well urge the parties to get together during the trial to agree as many of the small items as possible, to save time and expense.

If there are agreed photographs and plans of the place where the accident occurred, then these are shown to the judge so that by the time the first witness is called, he has an understanding of what the case is about.

Note that the judge is rarely told how much counsel thinks the claim is worth. Nor is the judge told if there has been any payment into court, nor the amount of any payment into court.

The witnesses are then called.

Witnesses: Unless written evidence has been agreed between the parties, the case almost always turns on the evidence given from the witness box. Normally the plaintiff (or pursuer), the person who has sustained the injury, is the first to give evidence, followed by other witnesses of fact, with expert evidence coming last. If the injuries were fatal, then the executors or administrators of the dead person's estate bring the action, and the legal team representing them will decide how best to prove liability by use of other witnesses.

Some plaintiffs cannot remember the accident because of head injury; but they may still be asked to confirm that they have no recollection, and then to give evidence about the *effect* of the injuries upon them.

A witness who is not an expert witness normally gives evidence without looking at his statement (called a 'proof of evidence'), although a document written immediately following an accident may be used to refresh the witness's memory. Counsel representing the plaintiff is responsible for asking the witness questions in such a way as to get the facts across to the judge. He must not 'lead' the witness on controversial issues. For example, counsel may say to the witness 'As you approached the crossroads, what happened?'

Counsel may *not* say 'Did the defendant driver shoot out of a side turning as you approached the crossroads?'

Witnesses can only give evidence that does not breach the 'hearsay' rule. So it will be acceptable if a witness says 'As I was walking down the High Street, about a month after the accident, I found that I was limping very badly.'

What the witness cannot say is 'I was talking to Gladys, my neighbour, and she told me that she had seen me limping in the High Street.'

The reason for this rule is that if the court is to know what Gladys saw, then the solicitor must arrange for her to come to the judge herself and give evidence. She can then be questioned about whether she is telling the truth or exaggerating, but if the witness tells the judge what Gladys said she saw, there is no opportunity to cross-examine.

The evidence which each witness gives on first being called is termed giving evidence 'in chief'.

Cross-examination: When a witness has finished giving evidence 'in chief', counsel for the defendant is entitled to cross-examine. If the evidence given by the witness appeared honest and straightforward, then counsel will be careful not to irritate the judge by hectoring or bullying the witness. If, however, a witness appears to have been shifty, dishonest or evasive, then an experienced counsel will take a fairly robust line in questioning, watching out for the judge's reaction.

Counsel for the defendant is not restricted to questions about the evidence which has already been given, but can open new topics, so long as they are relevant. This is when the defence starts to reveal how much information they have gathered together, perhaps from enquiry agents or from other persons. For example, if a plaintiff has just given evidence that he has not been able to go bopping at the local disco because of his leg injury, counsel cross-examining may 'put it' to the witness that on a certain day he visited a disco and was seen bopping with considerable agility. Counsel need not give the source of the information, but will be asking the witness to admit or deny that he went bopping.

Honest witnesses have little to fear from cross-examination, so long as they listen to the question and answer that question calmly and without trying to be clever, rude or evasive. A witness who does not understand a question should say so.

Re-examination: After cross-examination is concluded, counsel for the plaintiff has an opportunity to pick up points which have arisen in the cross-examination. Counsel cannot at this stage introduce fresh evidence which should have been given 'in chief' in the first place. The purpose of re-examination is to repair any damage to the case which may have occurred in cross-examination, and to clarify any grey areas, where, perhaps, ambiguous answers could be interpreted adversely.

At any time during the evidence the judge is entitled to ask questions. When counsel for each party asks a question, they usually already know the likely answer and plan their questioning accordingly, but the judge has no worries about putting a foot wrong in asking questions. The judge is not partisan, but is there to ensure that the right decision is made. Therefore any questions the judge asks are usually forceful and go right to the heart of the issues. Very often lawyers for both parties can pick up the way in which a judge's mind is running from the questions asked.

Expert witnesses: Expert witnesses may be consulting engineers retained perhaps to help work out the mathematics of a road accident—giving views on the speed at which each vehicle was moving, the visibility and the braking distances. Consulting engineers are normally only involved if there is a serious dispute about what occurred, and it is rare for their evidence to be agreed. Other experts are likely to be medical experts if the medical evidence has not been agreed.

Ordinary witnesses give evidence of *facts* and most do their best to tell the truth as they understand it. Expert witnesses are in a different category; their role is to convince a judge about matters of *opinion*. Most expert witnesses are genuine in putting forward their opinions, although undoubtedly there are some (medical experts, in particular) who are widely known to be sympathetic to insurance companies and who are invariably unsympathetic to the plaintiff. Called 'piper experts' because they play the tune of the insurers who have paid them, they often come in for severe cross-examination.

Anyone called as an expert witness is fair game for some heavy cross-examination. It is not at all unusual to see expert witnesses reduced to confusion by skilful questioning, and many a promising case has collapsed because an expert witness has done his homework incorrectly or has been less than impartial in his approach. For example, a high-powered medical expert once criticised the claimant's general practitioner for describing the condition in question as 'lumbago', saying that this was a general term used by doctors who don't know what is wrong with the patient's back. It was then revealed in cross-examination that the expert witness had himself described the condition as 'lumbago'!

As judges have to decide which of the conflicting expert opinions is to be preferred, such gaffes tend to cause much merriment in court and make life easier for the judge in deciding which expert view to accept.

Hostile witnesses: Nomally a witness is only called because the lawyers calling him or her know what the evidence to be given is likely to be. If that witness has already given a signed statement or has given evidence on oath in another court, but then, when called on this occasion, gives entirely contradictory evidence, counsel calling him or her can ask the judge for permission to treat that person as a 'hostile' witness.

If the judge agrees, then counsel is entitled to cross-examine his own witness about the apparent contradiction. If, however, a witness has never given a signed statement, or previous evidence, but has merely *said* to the solicitor in advance what his evidence is going to be, then there will be nothing on which to 'bite' if the witness does not say what is expected in the witness box. There has to be a signed statement or other recorded testimony in a previous court which is a matter of record before the hostile witness approach can be used. That is why solicitors obtain written and signed statements before trials.

Subpoena (pronounced 'sub-peener') witnesses: Many witnesses come to court simply because they are asked. But sometimes, the solicitor has to apply to the court before the trial and ask for a subpoena, which is an order of the court requiring the witness to attend. It is an offence to disobey. On the other hand, a subpoena may be necessary even where the witness *is* willing to co-operate; for example, police officers are not allowed to give evidence in civil cases unless a subpoena has been issued. In Scotland, the terminology is rather different, but the principle is much the same.

Closing the case: When counsel for the plaintiff has called the last witness and put in any permissible written evidence, he (or she) normally then tells the judge that he is closing the plaintiff's case. Once these magic words have been said, it is not normally possible for any further evidence to be called on behalf of the plaintiff.

The defendant's case: Counsel for the defendant then opens the defendant's case. There is rarely any introductory speech. Normally counsel simply calls the witnesses. These witnesses are dealt with 'in chief', in cross-examination by counsel for the plaintiff and then in re-examination, as described above.

The closing speeches: When all the evidence on behalf of the defendant has been given, counsel make their closing speeches, first counsel for the defendant, then counsel for the plaintiff. The speeches usually sum up the main points of the argument on each side, each side hoping to persuade the judge (if he has not already made up his mind!) in their favour.

Judgment: In a straightforward case a judge may be able to give judgment immediately. A more complex case may be adjourned for an hour or so, or perhaps until the next day, for the judge to consider and decide. In really difficult cases, judgment may be postponed for several weeks.

Listening to the judgment may be nerve-wracking—the judge meanders through the history of what happened and then makes 'findings of fact.' These are the facts which then determine the decision on matters of law which then follow, and indicate to the parties which evidence he has preferred on matters which were controversial. He may describe one witness as 'honest and straightforward' but another one as having 'an unreliable memory.' Rarely, he will lash out and describe a witness as 'a brazen liar.'

Having made the findings of fact, he then indicates that his conclusion on those facts is that one side or the other has won on the issue of liability. If he makes a finding that the plaintiff has proved his case, then he will deal with any question of contributory negligence.

Whether or not he has found in favour of the plaintiff on liability, the judge will normally then deal with general damages for pain and suffering and loss of amenity, before moving on to handicap on the labour market, loss of future earnings, and lastly turning to special damages.

At this point the lawyers on each side tot up the totals rapidly and do quick calculations about the interest to be added.

The judge then orders that judgment be entered for the successful party and asks to be addressed on the question of who should be responsible for the costs of the action. It is at this point that the judge's attention is drawn to any payment into court. If the total award to the plaintiff exceeds the amount paid into court, then the judge will order that the plaintiff be awarded his costs.

If the total award is less than the amount paid into court, the plaintiff has in effect lost. The judge will listen to arguments on costs but, almost invariably, will order that the taxed (ie vetted) costs of both sides incurred since the date of payment in, are paid by the plaintiff out of his damages.

Appeal: It is possible to appeal against the decision of a county court judge or a High Court judge. The grounds for doing so are limited, and are confined to questions of law, not findings of fact.

The
day
of
the
trial

In which Arthur learns that all the
world's a stage

Arthur and Jackie walked through the maze of corridors with Paul Bright, who was in his element, climbing steps here, leading them through the swing doors there, until they reached the passage outside the courtroom where Arthur's case was to be heard. Along the corridor they saw 'Buster' Keaton QC and Jeremy Sprigg. Arthur felt his heart racing as the reality of what he was undertaking became all too clear.

Before he'd left home he'd carefully parted his hair down the middle, smarming it down with water, so that he would look his best for the big day, not wanting the judge to think him scruffy. He'd also chosen his best blue suit, a red and white striped shirt and a blue tie with a starry pattern.

Now the Great Man, in his black gown and wig, approached and shook Arthur's hand. 'Morning Mr Henderson. Morning Paul. And this is Mrs Henderson? I'm delighted to meet you. This is Mr Jeremy Sprigg, my junior. I expect your husband has told you about him?'

'Thank you, yes,' said Mrs Henderson from beneath the large blue hat, which she'd bought for the occasion. As she spoke, her head was bowed so that only her mouth was visible underneath the brim.

The Great Man adjusted his battered grey wig, which lay on his head like a discarded dishcloth. 'Look, Paul, I've just had a word with the other side. I met their counsel in the robing room and I asked him what his game was. Told him that £65,000 was nonsense.'

'Good,' responded Paul Bright. 'And I see we've got Mr Justice Scoular taking the case. That won't do us any harm, will it?'

The Great Man shook his head. 'No. I've known Pongo Scoular for years. He led me once in a nasty animal case down in Bodmin. Nearly all Bodmin cases involve animals. But that's another story. Anyway, he'll play it straight down the middle. We needn't worry about Pongo, which is a point I made to the other counsel. I could see that he knew that £65,000 wasn't going to crack it and that he'd be doing dammed well to persuade Pongo to award less. I told him I'd take instructions on £85,000. I didn't say we'd *settle* for that. Just that I'd take instructions.'

Mrs Henderson retreated further behind her brim and stepped back a pace as the Great Man exhaled an air-polluting blast of cigar smoke. 'There's the opposition.' He nodded, looking down the corridor. 'The insurance man, the solicitor and the two counsel. The insurance man's the one with the calculator. I've seen him before. It's obvious they're re-doing their mathematics.' He smiled at Arthur, who did his best to look cheerful as yet another strand of wiry hair rose to the vertical.

'Whatever you do, Mr Henderson, keep looking cheerful,' said Keaton. 'The other side are going to be watching our reactions before we go into court. Just you see. The other barrister will come over in a minute for a word. He'll put forward an offer and then I'll tell you the figure. All you've got to do is just watch Paul Bright's reaction. He knows how to do it.' He grinned with twenty-five years experience. 'Whatever you do, don't look relieved that another offer has been made; don't look as if you're going to jump in the air with happiness.'

Those eyes, which had haunted Arthur since the consultation, fixed him again. 'Ever been an actor, Mr Henderson? I don't remember reading it in your proof of evidence. Well today's your day to be Sir Laurence Olivier. Ah! Here he comes rising like a trout with another offer. So don't forget what I said. All the world's a stage, not least when you're standing outside a courtroom door. They'll all be watching for your reaction, probably even trying to overhear what we say.'

With a flourish he spun on his heels, his long black gown swaying out behind him, as he joined the other Queen's Counsel and together they strolled down the corridor, hands deep in pockets, heads bowed, like a pair of vultures strutting towards the decaying corpse of another litigant.

'Come on Arthur, look cheerful,' encouraged Paul Bright. 'Do what Mr Keaton said. £65,000 is not enough and the insurers are worried. Just think what they must be feeling as they see your witnesses lined up.' He turned to Mrs Henderson and spoke to the brim of her hat. None of her face was visible. 'Why don't you get a cup of coffee downstairs? It's only ten o'clock. We shan't start till 10.30 and that assumes we don't reach a settlement in the next half an hour.'

The brim of Mrs Henderson's hat shook and, from somewhere beneath it, a muttered 'no' came forward. Paul was puzzled about why Mrs Henderson kept her head bowed. Was she really so intimidated by the occasion? But then he remembered her cosmetic surgery. So that was it. She was literally scared to show her face. He'd have to speak to Arthur about that when the case was over.

The pungent smell of cigar smoke heralded the return of the Great Man. 'They're offering £70,000. I told them it wasn't enough.' He looked at Paul. Arthur Henderson looked at Paul.

The solicitor shook his head vehemently in theatrical fashion. 'No. Far too low.' He spoke loudly, clearly so that his voice carried across the short distance to where the insurance group were huddled. 'There's no way that the case can settle at £70,000. Let's run it. I'm sure you'd agree, wouldn't you, Arthur?'

Arthur gulped, wishing he could just grab the cheque for £70,000 and disappear. Come on Arthur, he told himself, be like Sir Laurence Olivier. 'I agree,' his voice squeaked. He tried again. 'I'm not settling for that.' This time his voice was more positive.

'Right then. We're all agreed,' said Keaton. 'I don't think we should suggest a counter-offer. I'll reject the offer and we'll move a few feet further down the corridor and watch out for that calculator being used again and then perhaps we'll go 'walkies'. If by 10.29 there's nothing better than £70,000, Arthur can re-consider but, for the moment, I think we'll let them stew.' He turned to Paul. 'I'll talk to their counsel. Paul—you make arrangements to get all the witnesses brought into court. Jeremy—take Mr and Mrs Henderson into court and sit them down. We'll give the impression to the insurers that we're all ready to fight them. That should be worth a few thousand. I don't think we've had their last word yet.'

The Great Man moved away and the group broke up so that moments later, Arthur found himself sitting in the high vaulted courtroom, gazing up at the bench where he knew the judge would sit in less than half an hour, if the matter were not settled. He smiled at Jackie but, from beneath the wide brim, she saw nothing of the bulldog expression which he was putting on for the benefit of the insurers. Jeremy Sprigg decided to regale Arthur with the story of Pongo Scoular and the nasty animal case down in Bodmin—anything to distract Arthur Henderson from the agony which he was obviously suffering.

In the corridor, Paul Bright and 'Buster' Keaton were laughing too, for, almost surreptitiously, they'd seen the solicitor for the insurers produce his calculator, as if to check the figures yet again. 'I've done my maths,' said Paul. 'I value the claim at £81,708 plus costs.'

Keaton nodded. 'Sprigg and I did the figures last night. I put a bracket on it of £80,000/£85,000. So we're in the same area. I understand the insurers don't like the claims for the gardener, the shoes and the automatic car. We're not far apart on future loss of earnings or pain and suffering. It's these other continuing losses which they're jibbing about. They rattle up so quickly, those figures.'

Paul Bright produced his own calculations. (See page 130 for Paul's calculations.) 'Now they're re-doing their figures, let's get out of the way. What about going into court?'

A conspiratorial smile played on 'Buster' Keaton's lips. 'No. I don't want to overplay it. But I agree we shouldn't hang around here. Let's just wander off down the corridor and keep out of their way until nearer 10.30. Give them maximum aggro.'

They strolled down the corridor and out into the crisp morning air. 'I always think it's a good idea to get everyone else into court but, if I'm looking for a settlement, I prefer to stay outside,' said Keaton. 'Sometimes I might go into court if I'm convinced that negotiations are at an end, but otherwise I think it's best to do what we're doing and just keep out of the way. I'll finish my cigar and then we'll stroll back and go straight into the court. If they want to accost us, then of course we shall be ready to talk.'

At 10.27 am precisely they re-entered the building, strolling nonchantly down the tiled corridor, passing other groups of lawyers, each playing out their own one act dramas. This was the moment of truth. Would the insurers and their team have all gone into court, or had they decided to make another offer? There was no one there. For a moment Paul Bright thought that they had overplayed their hand. 'Doesn't look too promising, does it?' he said. 'Anyway, I can tell you that Arthur's bottom line is £75,000. Anything less than that and we fight. Those are my instructions and I've been through the position very carefully with him. Mind you, the way he looked this morning, I think he'd have settled for his bus fare home.'

'Poor blighter. I'm still worried about him as a witness. Oh well, too late for that. We'd better go in.' The Queen's Counsel pushed open the swing door and hurried forward to the front of the court where his clerk had laid out his reference books and papers neatly in a line. The list of authorities, the cases to which he would refer, had been handed in to the usher and now, on the Bench, were identical books, so that the judge would be able to refer to them during the course of the trial.

Keaton shuffled sideways into his row and checked his notes. He was just about to sit down to await the judge's entrance when there was a voice in his ear. He looked to his side and it was the Queen's Counsel for the insurance company. '£77,500 and not a penny more.'

'No! £80,000, plus costs to be taxed, an order for legal aid taxation and an order for payment of money out of court.' Keaton had his response at his fingertips.

'Done.'

'Then we are agreed.' Keaton leant forward to where Paul Bright was disappearing beneath a mountain of photographs, plans and endless documentation, making sure that there were copies of everything to be produced during the trial. 'It's settled at £80,000. You'd better tell the client.' He watched as Bright slid out of his seat and spoke to Arthur Henderson, who was not sure on this occasion which role Sir Laurence Olivier was playing.

'We've done well. It's all over Arthur. The formalities in front of the judge will only take five minutes and then we can all go home.'

'Oh, I see.' Arthur felt confused and ran his hands over his hair, flattening it down as best he could. He felt sticky and uncomfortable. It would take a while to sink in. He'd lived with this for so long.

There is a well tested legal maxim that 'a bad settlement is better than a good case', but Arthur did even better than that—he got a *good* settlement out of his good case. The moral of this story is that a bird in the hand is worth two in the bush, in matters of law as in everything else. It could have gone wrong if Arthur's case had been argued out in court. There is no certainty in litigation. The best solicitor and the best counsel can find their plans go wrong—perhaps because of an awkward judge, a bad witness or an unexpected development. Perhaps this is why over 90% of compensation cases are settled without going to court.

The million pound claim

In July 1987, for the first time in England, an award of damages for personal injuries exceeded £1,000,000. How did the plaintiff achieve this sum? The answer is that the injuries and their effect were truly catastrophic.

Samer Aboul-Hosn was nearly nineteen in September 1982, when he underwent an operation for the removal of a cyst from his brain. Judgment was eventually given against the trustees of the hospital in question, who had denied liability.

After the operation, a scan revealed that problems had developed and there was progressive deterioration of Samer's condition. The consequence was irreversible brain damage and nineteen year old Samer had his life ruined almost beyond comprehension. His mental age was reduced to that of a two year old but without any chance of improvement. He could not speak. His eyesight was damaged. At better moments now he can respond slowly to simple instructions to stand or sit. There is perhaps some understanding of other instructions. He has fits of affection and temper. He can walk, but not naturally. Feeding is difficult and he needs help to go to the lavatory.

Samer will need constant help for the rest of his life, twenty-four hours a day. Contrast this with the nineteen year old who had achieved four 'A' levels and a place at university and who would have pursued a successful career. Worst of all, the medical evidence suggested that poor Samer may have some understanding of his own predicament, a thought which must haunt not only him but all who now read of the life he is leading.

How was the total award reached?

Pain suffering and loss of amenities £85,000

Cost of past care and expenditure by parents   £100,700
(The judge assessed the true value of the
high degree of care by the parents at £16,137
per year. Samer's father had given up his job
to look after his son.)

Future care £400,800
(The judge took a multiplier of seventeen
years. Careful analysis was made of the cost
of care at home, the cost of care in a residen-
tial care home and the cost of rehabilitative
treatment at a special unit.)

Housing needs £48,100

Future loss of earnings (including a car) £331,000
(The evidence was that Samer would prob-
ably have become a chemical engineer. The
judge had expert evidence available about
expected level of earnings and added the loss
of the benefit of a company car from the
time when Samer would have been thirty.)

Court of Protection fees £34,500
(This is the cost of having the damages
managed by the Court of Protection
because Samer was in no position to look
after his own damages.)

Interest on damages £31,550

	Total	£1,032,000

The damages were worked out on the basis that if Samer lives as long as is expected, then the capital sum awarded, and the income from it, will, over the period of his lifetime, all be spent. If Samer dies unexpectedly early, then the damages will prove to have been too much. If he lives longer than expected, the money may well run out. As the damages are awarded on a once and for all basis, there is no going back for more. In cases like this, as much as 75% of the award can relate to the cost of future care and the long-term loss of earnings. There are many imponderables and there is bound to be some element of speculation in a claim involving views of the cost of future care and loss of earnings. The court can only do its best, judged in the context of previous decisions and the evidence put before the court. In Samer's case the court was much helped by a video which conveyed to the judge Samer's daily life.

By contrast with this tragic case, Arthur's difficulties pale almost into insignificance. But here, very briefly indeed, is how Paul Bright valued Arthur's claim and came to the conclusion that the right amount of compensation would be £81,708:

Pain and suffering and loss of amenity £18,000
Interest £900
                                                        ———
                                                        £18,900

Handicap on the labour market if Arthur
were to lose his job £3,000
Future loss of earnings £30,000
Cost of gardener now Arthur can't do his
own garden £9,000

Cost of outside contractors, garage mech-
anics etc to do jobs Arthur used to be able to
do himself £7,500
Extra cost of car with automatic trans-
mission £4,500
Cost of special shoes £1,125
Loss of earnings from date of accident
to trial £4,450
Travelling expenses, phone calls etc £350
Cost of gardener to date of trial £1,150
Cost of shoes to date of trial £200
Clothing damaged in accident £75
Excess under Arthur's motor policy £50

Total special damages to date of trial £6,625
Interest on special damages £1,058

GRAND TOTAL   £81,708

A fairy godmother (also known as the Motor Insurers' Bureau)

Usually, when an accident occurs on the road, there is an insurer to pay compensation to the person injured. Unfortunately, though, this is not always so. Pedal cyclists, for example, are not obliged to be insured and usually are not, although their carelessness may cause serious injury. Other examples of situations where there is no insurance cover are where the driver at fault does not stop and is not found (a 'hit and run' case) or where the driver at fault has no insurance (this is, of course, an offence).

In a case like this, you may have a perfectly good claim in law for thousands of pounds, but unless the other person has the money, it is probably not worth pursuing the claim. Indeed, legal aid would not be granted to pursue a fruitless case.

Happily, a body known as the Motor Insurers' Bureau ('MIB') will meet claims for personal injury in some of these cases. Note that the MIB is not responsible for providing compensation for damage to *vehicles*. It will only consider cases of bodily injury sustained in a road traffic accident, but if that condition is met, it will then pay compensation for loss of earnings, but not out of pocket expenses such as the replacement of damaged clothes. The MIB may insist that the claimant seek compensation from any other driver who may have been partly to blame.

The MIB is not a charitable institution. It was set up and is financed by the insurance industry, and it operates within very strict guidelines which must be followed precisely.

The address of the Motor Insurers' Bureau is New Garden House, 78 Hatton Garden, London EC1N 8JW (tel: (01) 242 0033).

Medical
negligence

In which Jackie Henderson is distressed

Paul Bright was not looking forward to the meeting. His secretary appeared, leading Arthur and Jackie Henderson. Jackie was in a new blue suit which Arthur had bought her with his damages, but the hat she had worn to the trial was gone, so that Paul could see her face. He knew that she was nearly forty but she looked ten years older than Arthur. As he shook hands, he noticed that she kept her eyes cast down, as if ashamed of looking at him.

He waited whilst coffee and biscuits were laid out, before asking Arthur 'How does it feel, now that it's over?'

'It's a great weight off my shoulders,' Arthur replied, 'but now I'm only concerned for Jackie.'

The solicitor turned to her, smiling reassuringly. 'Arthur's told me the background. I'll do what I can, but it won't be easy.'

Eyes still looking at the Wilton carpet, Jackie nodded in embarrassment. 'I've been such a fool. Vanity, I suppose you would call it. It's just that I felt that . . . I was getting very wrinkled. Quite beyond my years. Then I saw an advert in a magazine and so I started saving until I'd raised the £1,800 to pay for the operation.'

'Plenty of people have it done. Facelifts are pretty commonplace. If it was important to you then . . . it was probably the right thing. What did your GP say about it?' Paul Bright remembered recommending to Arthur that he get his wife to see the GP before the operation.

'Said I was making a fuss about nothing.' Jackie Henderson studied her fingers, speaking slowly. 'Here, you'd better see some pictures of me as I was.' She thrust a clutch of photographs at him, showing her sitting in the garden and wearing a funny hat at a

Christmas party. Paul Bright studied them carefully. It was extraordinary. She looked fifteen years younger before the operation. He then looked up at her as she answered the unasked question. 'They were all taken last year.' She started to cry and mopped her eyes with a small white handkerchief, before rapidly composing herself. 'I'm sorry. I've been very stupid. I can see you're shocked. I look older than ever now, don't I?'

Paul Bright *was* shocked and so he thought carefully before replying. 'Well, it certainly wasn't the result it should have been.'

Arthur chipped in, just as the solicitor was about to continue. 'Look. It just has to be said. Jackie does look older.' He fumbled in his pocket and produced the advertisement. 'There's the headline. "Simple, fast, safe cosmetic surgery. Take years off your face. Be young again. It's cheaper than you think".'

Paul nodded thoughtfully. 'And I look at least fifty now, don't I?' said Jackie. It was very much a statement. Furthermore, it was true.

'So, let me just summarize. You saw an advert. You went to see this consultant in Harley Street who agreed to do the job. What explanations did he give? Did he warn you that things could go wrong? When dealing with negligence of professional people, just because something doesn't turn out quite as well as expected, doesn't necessarily mean that there's a claim. Cosmetic surgeons have to use reasonable care and skill. If they do that and the outcome is not as good as it should be, then you probably don't have a case. What we shall have to do is to examine what advice he gave you, what he led you to believe he could achieve, and what consent form you signed.'

'You don't sound very hopeful. That's not a bit like you.' It was Arthur speaking.

'Just say that I'm being cautious. Of all the claims against professional people, those against the medical profession are the hardest to prove. The courts have taken quite a robust view, as a matter of public policy, to protect the medical profession from the type of trigger-happy litigation which they face in the USA.' He walked to the window and shut it with a satisfying bang to keep out the rain which was beating down on Croydon High Street. 'Proving blame is far from easy, even assuming that you can get other members of the medical profession to come forward and say that a reasonable standard of care was not met.'

'Why?' Jackie's hands were still shaking.

'One reason is that the medical profession can seem rather small. If you want to sue a brain surgeon, you find that most of them know each other, which means it's an embarrassment for them to give evidence against one of their pals. Others simply have an aversion to the legal profession and claims generally, and will do nothing to help. Some believe it's their duty to support their colleagues through thick and thin. In plastic surgery, it's a small field. Happily, by the sound of it, the person who did your job may not be one of the magic circle of leading plastic surgeons. Particularly with these private outfits who advertise in magazines, many don't have the experience to undertake this sort of work at all. If so, I can probably find a specialist who will help.'

'And legal aid?' enquired Arthur.

'You're joking! With your £80,000 of damages? They take into consideration the spouse's means, so it's just a waste of time applying. So I'm afraid that every penny you spend on me and medical consultants is at your expense unless and until the case is strong enough to persuade the other side to settle the claim and pay the costs. By the way, who did your operation?'

'Trevor Finney,' Jackie replied.

'Don't know him,' said Paul Bright. 'Anyway, you'd better show me your documentation. I suppose you did give your written consent?'

'Oh yes. I had half an hour with him, talking it over and then he gave me this document which sets out what he was going to do. I signed it, as you can see.'

With much muttering, tut-tutting and sharp intakes of breath, Paul read the document. 'What you signed indicates that everything has been properly explained to you and that you understood that he could give no guarantees of success. He described the nature of the operation. The operation was to tighten the skin around your jaw-line and neck and to remove fat which had collected under your chin. I gather you also wanted the bags of skin around your eyes removed. He made quite clear that this document was the sole contract between you. He didn't warrant that you would look younger, prettier, sexier or even different at all. What's more, he also pointed out that in all cosmetic surgery there is a risk of failure and that, while he would do his best, nevertheless, the result might not be as good as you or he would want.' Paul Bright shook his head from side to side. 'Did you understand all that when you signed the document?'

'Well . . .' stammered Jackie. 'I suppose I did. I didn't think much, didn't take much notice. Anyway, what happened was that the scars have stretched so that the skin sagged and flopped all round my cheeks as you can see.'

'Anyway,' chipped in Arthur, rather boldly for him, 'I thought it was illegal to limit your responsibility for personal injury?' He sat back, arms folded, looking rather smug in a way which he'd never done when *he'd* been the client. 'I heard that on the radio.' he added by way of explanation.

'True, but Mr Finney hasn't. All he did was lay out the ground rules. Indeed, far from saying you cannot sue him, he is saying 'go on, sue me if it goes wrong but these terms are the terms on which I agreed to undertake the operation.' Jackie had it all explained to her and went ahead.'

Jackie was about to say something but couldn't bring herself to do it. Tears started to flow and Paul Bright's heart went out to her. He'd seen this before—all too often. A stream of clients who had come to grief over cosmetic surgery. For some he'd been successful, but it was never easy.

Arthur put his arm round his wife's shoulders. 'Don't distress yourself. I've told you before. You look fine to me and, even if you didn't . . . I'd still love you.' He leant across and kissed his wife on the cheek, whilst Paul offered a box of tissues.

Paul Bright waited until the sobbing had stopped. 'What I'm going to do is to invite the clinic and Mr Finney to produce the medical records. It's reasonable to give them six weeks to do this because he'll have to get consent from his Defence Union. If I haven't got the records at the end of six weeks, I then make an application to the court for an order that the medical records be produced, which almost invariably succeeds.' He smiled reassuringly at Jackie Henderson. 'Don't worry. You won't have to attend. This is something which I deal with on the basis of a sworn statement. Armed with the medical records, we can then get an opinion from our own consultant. If Mr Finney has carried out the operation without following the proper standards, then we'll get him. It's as simple as that . . . but what happened to you may be sheer bad luck.'

When going to see a solicitor about a medical neg-ligence case, you should have ready all the 'basic facts' set out on page 29, and the answers to these questions:

- for what condition were you being treated?

- who were the specialist and GP involved?

- which hospital (if any) carried out the treatment?

- what consent did you give?

- what explanation, if any, was given to you about the treatment, its likely outcome and the risk of side effects or the risk of failure?

- who gave that explanation?

- were there any witnesses to the explanation?

- on what date do you think the mistake or mistakes were made?

- what mistakes do you think were made?

- has anyone admitted a mistake?

- have you made any formal or informal complaint about your treatment?

- do you have any correspondence?

- have you received any written or oral explanation from the hospital, consultant or other doctor commenting about the position? If so from whom?

Special problems in medical cases

If your claim is for medical negligence, it is even more important than ever to choose a solicitor who is familiar with that type of claim, because it calls for even more specialist expertise than other accident cases. If you have difficulty finding a specialist, the best course is to write, as soon as possible, to Action for the Victims of Medical Accidents, 24 Southwark Street, London SE1 1TY (tel: (01) 403 4744). This excellent charity is overburdened with requests for help and you may have to wait to hear from them. It is worth waiting—but do not allow a time limit for pursuing your claim to expire while you are waiting for a response. The *basic* time limit is three years.

The task of proving that a doctor or consultant has been negligent is on the claimant. As in other cases of negligence, the claimant has to show, 'on the balance of probabilities', that the treatment was negligent. This means that it has to be shown that, more likely than not, the treatment fell below an acceptable medical standard of care. This is the difficulty for the claimant. The courts do not expect the medical profession to perform to a standard of care that is anything like perfection. Accordingly, any number of disastrous consequences of medical treatment can leave the victim without any legal remedy.

The test applied by the courts is:

> 'Has the medical practitioner acted in accordance with a practice accepted as proper by a responsible body of medical men, skilled in that particular art, even although a body of adverse opinion also exists among medical men.'

Put into English, this means that if you suffer an adverse consequence from medical treatment, then you will have no remedy if the doctor who treated you can call other members of his profession to say that they would have done the same thing.

If the courts (as in other situations) were to adopt an *objective* stance as to what was reasonable in medical matters, then the chances are that many more people would receive compensation for what are rightly regarded as medical mistakes.

Another difficulty in these cases is obtaining the medical records to assess whether or not there is a claim worth pursuing. Whilst a patient cannot demand to have his records, most health authorities will now agree to release them to a nominated medical adviser or to a solicitor (and it ought to be to the solicitor), so long as there are legitimate grounds for suggesting that the release of the records is justified. In the absence of co-operation, the solicitor has to apply to the court for an order to inspect them or have copies.

Information about the risks of treatment is another problem area. Patients who ask about a proposed treatment *ought* to be entitled to a proper explanation. Unfortunately the courts have not given clear guidance on the topic. It is therefore difficult for solicitors to advise whether or not a patient has been adequately informed about the nature of the treatment undertaken. One important decision suggested that a patient does have the right to be informed; on the other hand, another case has indicated that the doctor must judge what the patient should be told, concluding that it is not for the courts to decide just what the patient should

142

be told. The dilemma is a genuine one. Patients should have sufficient information to enable a sensible decision to be taken without being put in fear of undergoing necessary treatment.

It is likely that the present law is that, unless there is some powerful reason for not doing so, a doctor must, before beginning treatment, volunteer a warning where there is *a substantial risk of serious consequences*. The doctor must give a warning in circumstances where responsible medical opinion considers it proper to do so.

Sterilization is a common area for litigation. It also highlights the dilemma faced by doctors. Patients should normally be told of the small but important risk of failure to achieve sterility; yet, in contrast, they should also be told that successful sterilization is expected to be permanent and not reversible.

Medical negligence claims most often arise out of sterilization cases; obstetrics and gynaecology; anaesthetics and cosmetic surgery.

Because of the difficulties in obtaining compensation for medical mistakes, there is pressure for reform. It is suggested that victims should all receive something, even if it were far less than can be obtained by those able to prove negligence under the present law. It is a complex problem, which requires much careful consideration.

The medical evidence arrives

In which Jackie has mixed fortunes

Jackie and Arthur Henderson sat opposite Paul Bright, who was quick to notice that she had changed her hairstyle so that her long black hair was now combed in front of her ears, helping to hide some of the lines and folds which had gathered since the failed operation. A glance was sufficient to confirm what Arthur had privately told him. Jackie was now in a state of depression. He knew that she was taking sleeping pills and was fearful of going out, imagining that people were laughing at her.

'It's nearly four months now since we last met, isn't it?' The solicitor opened what he knew was going to be a difficult interview. The look on his face showed his disgust at the delay and he waved a hand towards the thick bundle of papers. 'These are the medical records from the clinic. Unfortunately they were awkward about releasing them and I had to get an order from the court which meant a delay of nine weeks, waiting for a hearing. This only lasted two minutes because the other side didn't even resist. I'm afraid they just wanted to cause delay, and grind you down. That happens all too often. Anyway, the records arrived and I went through them. At least they were complete, or seemed to be. Sometimes vital pages are missing, sometimes whole sections of records inexplicably disappear. Sometimes I'm suspicious that whole pages have been re-written to cover up for mistakes. That's why I always read the records myself.'

Jackie nodded, eyes lowered as usual. 'And you've got the first independent report?'

'Yes. Mr Nippon-Tuck is one of the leading cosmetic specialists in London. He's always very sympathetic when operations go wrong and doesn't give a damn about criticising his colleagues if it's justified. Anyway, his report made clear that Mr

Finney could not be blamed. All the correct procedures were followed and what happened to you was sheer bad luck. That's why I asked if you'd like another opinion.'

'Which naturally we did,' said Arthur.

'Quite right. Mind you, I wasn't too hopeful in the light of Mr Nippon-Tuck's views, but anyway, I sent all the papers to James McNab, who's done a great deal of work for me. His report is full of sympathy but concludes that there's not a shred of support for allegations of negligence.' He picked up the document and scanned through to the last paragraph, which was the final opinion. 'What he says is that Mr Finney used all reasonable care and skill and that the techniques he used, the advice he gave, was in accordance with good practice. He'd warned you that a first class result could not be guaranteed. I'm afraid you're one of the few cases where the result is not as good as it should be, but no one is to blame.' As he spoke, Paul watched for Jackie's reaction. There was none. Just the lifeless eyes staring down and the clenching and re-clenching of her left fist round a crumpled blue tissue.

'It's so unfair. Finney's got away with it. Sheer butchery.' Arthur was making up for his wife's listlessness. 'So what do we do?' he asked. 'Get another report?'

The solicitor shook his head. 'You've spent £350 on medical reports, and another £450 on my firm's charges. We might be lucky and find another specialist who would support you but it would be just too easy for the other side to get batteries of doctors lined up to give evidence to show that there was no blame. Without legal aid you'd have to pay both sides' costs of the trial if you lost. And you *will* lose on the basis of this evidence.'

Arthur looked at Paul. 'So it's Plan B then, is it?'

There was a flicker of reaction from Jackie, who looked slightly puzzled.

Paul nodded. 'That seems to me to be far better. I think you should tell Jackie.'

'You see dear, Paul phoned me this morning and told me the news would be bad. We could spend £25,000 on litigation, fighting the clinic for days on end and still lose. So Paul suggested it was better that we spend some of my damages on having the operation re-done by Mr McNab. Paul spoke to him and, whilst there are no guarantees, he thinks he can put right the damage. If it costs two or three thousand, who cares about the expense? It's *your* happiness that counts and anyway, it's far cheaper than this litigation.'

'I don't think I could take another operation. I couldn't, I couldn't!'

'Well, the choice is yours,' said the solicitor gently. 'Mr McNab really is a good man. If he feels he can get it right, I think you should do it. What Arthur doesn't know is that I've spoken to James McNab again and, because you're so upset . . .' Bright picked his words carefully, avoiding the use of the word 'depressed' . . . 'he could take you in tomorrow. He's that keen to help. I think Arthur's right. You ought to go ahead.'

A watery smile flickered round Jackie's lips. 'Thank you. Perhaps I will.'

Having your say

Often all that is wanted by a person who has been let down by the medical profession is an explanation or an apology. Sometimes, perhaps because of pressures of work, but often out of high-handedness or arrogance, consultants treat victims with scant regard or indifference. Frustration at being unable to get explanations from consultants pushes many people into litigation, hoping to be able to find the truth, irrespective of compensation.

However, the reality is that, if there are strong grounds of complaint amounting to negligence, the litigation is more likely to be settled without going to court, so that any opportunities for questioning the consultant will never arise.

Those wishing to make a complaint, rather than pursue a claim for damages, have several courses of action open to them.

Complaints about non-clinical matters such as nursing care, cleanliness in hospitals and standards of food should be made in writing to the relevant health authority. The authority must respond with a letter of explanation. If this is not accepted, then the patient may refer the matter to the Health Service Commission (or 'Health Ombudsman'), Church House, Great Smith Street, London, SW1P 3BW (tel: (01) 212 7676), who will investigate and prepare a report. The Ombudsman will not investigate a matter which ought properly to be dealt with through the courts, neither can he deal with complaints involving clinical judgement. He cannot investigate the actions of GPs, dentists, opticians or pharmacists (see below).

A patient making a complaint about a clinical matter, for example whether or not surgery should have been carried out, or whether it was properly carried out, has a three phase procedure to go through. First, the patient refers the complaint to the consultant in charge, who should discuss it with the patient. If still dissatisfied, the complaint should be put in writing to the consultant, who informs the Regional Medical Officer (RMO). The consultant then discusses the position with colleagues and the RMO and sees the complainant once again. However, if the consultant feels that a meeting would not be useful, then the patient cannot insist on it.

Finally, if the patient remains unconvinced, then the RMO can arrange for an independent professional review. If the RMO decides, on enquiry, that legal action by the patient is possible, then the patient will be asked to give an undertaking not to litigate, in return for the independent review. It is worth noting that this element of the procedure has been criticised as unfair. The complainant, if dissatisfied with the way in which the RMO is handling the position, can complain to the Ombudsman. The independent professional review means that the complainant will normally have a meeting with two independent medical consultants who report their finding to the RMO (not to the complainant). A written report of the conclusions will then be submitted to the patient by the health authority.

The independent review phase of the investigation can be replaced by an inquiry, normally set up by the health authority. In exceptional cases a lawyer can be brought in to chair such an inquiry. Calls for this type of inquiry are often made, but rarely answered.

Complaints against GPs and dentists are made to the local Family Practitioner Committee (FPC). The FPC investigates complaints about, for example, the standard of care exercised by a GP, but will not concern itself with a complaint that the GP's receptionist is a dragon (a frequent complaint!). Again, there are three stages in the procedure. The address of the local FPC is in the telephone book.

The factory accident

In which Mr Ponder sees an apparition

'Wayne Henderson to see you Mr P,' said Doris the receptionist, her voice full of disapproval.

The door opened and the fat, bespectacled face of William Torquil Ponder peered round it. He did a double-take, eyes blinking in disbelief as he looked at young Wayne. 'You'd better come in, er Shane, er Wayne.' He was anxious to get the apparition out of the waiting room in case it scared the old ladies to death before he'd finished their wills.

Wayne followed the waddling Ponder down the dimly lit corridor. 'Do sit down and I suggest you put your crash helmet on the floor.'

'Not much room for it on your desk and that's for sure,' retorted Wayne breezily, as he seated himself across the desk from Mr Ponder, who was already surreptitiously taking a pill for his high blood pressure. He felt an attack coming on as he took in the changes since Wayne's last visit. The shoulder length black hair had now gone. Dressed now from head to foot in black, Wayne had gone gothic, or was it punk with a shaven head? Mr Ponder wasn't sure. The stud in the side of his nose was also disconcerting.

'I'm sure you won't mind me mentioning it Wayne but, if your case does go to court, I think you should dress a little more conventionally if you want to impress the judge.'

'Oh yeah? You mean him in the tatty wig, a red coat, a bunch of flowers. I've been to the courts. On a school outing. I've seen them. Do me a favour Mr P. At least I don't look like a poofter.'

'No, that I grant you,' Ponder hastily backtracked, wishing that Wayne's legal aid application had been rejected. But that would have been hoping for too much because, in truth, Wayne had a good case.

Three months before, Wayne had called in to talk

to Ponder about his claim, following his accident at work. Ponder had tried, God how he'd tried, to persuade Wayne to cross the road to consult Paul Bright, but all to no avail. 'There's no way I'm using Dad's brief. I do my own thing, don't I?' Wayne had said on that occasion as he rolled the thinnest of cigarettes with a Rizla. At the time, Mr Ponder had had his suspicions about what Wayne was smoking, a fear compounded when he asked 'Got any Coke Mr P?'

'Coke?' The voice was aghast. 'Dear dear me! Oh no! And please don't get involved in that sort of thing. Certainly not in my office anyway.'

'Nah! Turnit off! Pepsi, mate. I've got such a thirst. The old tonsils are clogged with all the grime from the South Circular.'

Ponder's blood pressure subsided momentarily. 'Doris makes a good cup of tea.'

'Thanks but no thanks. Anyway. Can't hang around long. I'm taking a new bird down to Brighton on the 750.'

'Then you've plenty of time before your train,' said Mr Ponder, looking at his watch. 'It's only 4.15.'

'Nah! 750—me bike! Anyway, what's all this legal aid? Sounds like a disease you catch in offices like this.' Wayne cackled at his own joke.

Ponder swallowed hard. This Henderson family would be the death of him. 'Well you've got it, legal aid that is. Let me just re-cap. You had your accident when you were seventeen. That was in October, 1984.' He searched for his notes, diving into the sea of confusion on his desk. 'Yes. I see. That was two and a half years ago, wasn't it?'

'Yeah! I'm nineteen and a half. So what happens now? Do I get my money or my old age pension first?

Ponder coughed nervously, thought about it for a

moment and then prevaricated. 'These claims are very slow-moving but I think we'll get your damages before you retire.' He didn't sound altogether certain. 'You do have a good case. Counsel says so.' Ponder himself had no idea whether the case was good or bad. 'When you were seventeen and your hair was long, it got caught in the rollers in the plastic extruding machine at work. Your right ear got into the rollers before some dear boy switched it off?'

'Yeah! A mate pressed the emergency button. I couldn't reach it.'

Mr Ponder smiled for the first time as a wicked thought crossed his mind: a bit of Wayne's ear was even now moulded into the fabric of someone's washing-up bowl.

'Since your legal aid arrived I've taken advice from counsel.' He flourished an important looking document. 'Counsel shares my view,' he said with presumption. 'Says you've got a good case, arising from breach of Section 14 of the Factories Act. And a claim for negligence too.'

'Negligence. Oh yeah! That jargon! Dad's always going on about that at home. No blame, no claim.'

Ponder played with his moustache as he flicked over the pages of the advice. To him this was a new and complex bit of the law, made by Parliament in 1961, long after he'd been to law school. 'Counsel says that you won't have to prove blame because your injuries were sustained as a result of breach of statutory duty. All you're going to have to prove is that your hair was dragged into a machine by moving parts. They have to be guarded. As they were not, you are bound to win.'

Ponder beamed in happiness. He and his client were learning at the same pace, but only he knew that. 'So there we are. I'll write to the insurers and get a meeting set up. They're bound to admit liability. Then we'll get a medical report and try to value the claim.' He was still paraphrasing counsel's advice. Ponder pointed towards his client's ear. 'You're obviously not embarrassed about it, your injury I mean. With that hairstyle, the missing chunk is quite obvious.'

'Nah! I'm proud ot it. It's a status symbol. Like I'm a war hero without having fought.' Wayne leant forward to give Ponder a knowing wink. 'Great for pulling the birds. Know what I mean? Which reminds me, must be moving on. Got to pick up Sharon in a minute. Anyway, Mr P, just so long as everything's all right.' Wayne picked up his helmet and clomped his way to the door, puffing little billows of dust from the fading red Axminster as he went.

'I'll let you know when there's something to report,' said Mr Ponder. Already he had decided that, in future, he'd try to deal with this client by telephone. The solicitor closed the door behind the disappearing client, who was whistling his way down the corridor. Ponder sat down at his desk and took another pill, all the while sniffing the air. Funny smell of burning. Didn't smell like cigarettes. Funny! It was getting worse. He got up and clambered over the stacks of files to the other side of the desk. Wayne's cigarette was smouldering on the Last Will and Testament of Emily Braithwaite.

Accidents at work

Mr Ponder, having taken counsel's advice, was correct in his observations about the law in factories. In accidents on the road, the claimant has to prove blame (negligence). In *some* factory accidents blame still has to be proved, but the rule of 'strict liability' has now been introduced in some situations in factories. In these circumstances blame does not have to be proved at all, the claimant only having to show that he has suffered loss caused by the person being sued in the manner alleged. The classic example is the obligation of a company to ensure that machinery is adequately guarded, so that operatives cannot come into contact with moving parts. The employer cannot defend himself by showing that he has taken reasonable care. The mere fact that the employee manages to become involved with moving parts, of itself, gives rise to a claim.

Nevertheless, if the employee himself has not taken reasonable care, then the courts can apportion blame. Indeed, it is possible that the carelessness of the employee is so bad that, whilst the employer can be found liable for breach of the strict duty laid down, nevertheless the employee receives no compensation because his own disregard for his personal safety contributed 100% to the situation which developed.

Most employers have to keep an accident book, recording accidents which occur. These records can be very important evidence when a claim is made. Far too often, employees do not ensure that their accident is *accurately* recorded. For example, you, as the victim of an accident, may know that you tripped over a hole in a carpet before falling. Someone else, completing the entry on your behalf, may simply write 'fell.' The vital factor is *why* you tripped, but that information has not been recorded.

If you are not in a position to complete the accident book yourself, try to ensure that the entry is, nevertheless, accurate. Better still, keep a note of the words which you want to be recorded, get them recorded and continue to use that form of wording consistently in all documents. All too often, contradictions arise between what has been written in the accident book and other forms completed when claiming State benefits or in describing to doctors how the accident occurred. Credibility can easily be lost by such contradictions.

If you are unfortunate enough to have an accident at work, here are some do's and don'ts for you:

- DO identify witnesses so that your solicitor can get statements while matters are fresh in their mind.

- DO register the accident as an industrial accident at your local social security office and claim any state benefits due to you.

- DO make a sketch plan of the place where the accident occurred, in case your employers change the layout.

- DO notify your trade union, if you are a member, as most unions will instruct the union solicitor to put in the claim for you.

- DON'T enter into correspondence with your employer about the accident without taking advice.

Before seeing a solicitor about an accident at work, gather together the information set out on page 29, and the answers to these questions:

- how did your accident occur?

- were there any witnesses and are they prepared to give statements?

- why do you think your employer was to blame?

- do you have any photographs or were any photographs taken? If so, bring them with you.

- do you have a sketch plan of the place where the accident occurred?

- did your employer make an investigation into the accident and, if so, what did you say and what was the conclusion, if known to you?

- did you fill in the accident report book? If not, was it completed by someone else and what did it say?

- did your employer report the circumstances of the accident to the DHSS?

- has anyone else had an accident like yours in similar circumstances? Give details.

- has your employer changed the system of work as a result of your accident?

- if you are a union member, what steps has your union taken on your behalf?

The amount of damages, tactics and procedure for pursuing a claim like Wayne's are similar to those in Arthur Henderson's claim arising out of a road accident.

The law about accidents at work is broadly similar in England & Wales and Scotland, although there are some minor subtle differences.

Time
and
tide
wait
for
no
one

In which Mr Ponder feels as sick as a parrot

Mr Ponder feels sick

Even his chocolate biscuit didn't taste as good as usual today. William Torquil Ponder was a worried man. He'd read and re-read the letter from the insurers who represented Wayne's employers. He looked at it again and blinked behind those large black glasses. 'As the writ was issued more than three years after the accident, we must advise you that the claim by your client is statute-barred. Under no circumstances will we meet this claim, even if, which is not admitted, your client could prove any liability.'

He looked at the date on the letter and saw that it had been lying in the clutter in front of him for nearly four months as he'd wondered what to do. He walked round the room. 'Oh dear!' he muttered to himself as he saw the baleful look of Ebenezer Ponder, his late father, in the oil painting by the window. It was 4.30 p.m. and Wayne Henderson was due to arrive any minute. It was his duty to tell him that he had no claim. 'Dear oh dear,' he shook his head. He'd been . . . negligent—hadn't started the proceedings in time. He shuddered, reached for the blood pressure pills and jumped nervously as the phone rang.

'Your client is here, Mr P.'

With a sigh, Ponder skirted the charred remains of Emily Braithwaite's Last Will and Testament and went to meet the client. Down in the waiting room, he managed a wan smile, though Wayne's appearance made it disappear rapidly. How could such a nice man as Arthur have produced something like this, he wondered.

'Follow me, er, Shane,' said Ponder and Wayne did so. Today he was wearing a sleeveless black waistcoat with a Michael Jackson motif, black knuckle-duster gloves and thigh boots with metal clasps running up the sides. If these were disconcerting to Mr Ponder, they were nothing compared with the large blue parrot which was sitting on Wayne's shoulder.

'How do you like my new bird?' said Wayne with a grin. 'Nah! Only joking. Still got the same little raver. Matter of fact, this is Sharon's parrot, only they don't like her taking it to the Social Security office. I knew you wouldn't mind me bringing him in. Answers to the name of Elvis.'

'Quite, quite,' said Ponder, his mind miles away.

'Anyway, Mr P—how's the claim? Got the damages yet?' He leaned back and put a boot on the corner of Ponder's desk.

'Not exactly. I'm afraid the insurers have denied liability and said your claim, the writ I mean, was too late.'

'What's that mean, in English like?'

'It means your claim had to be started within three years of the accident, by issuing the writ. Unfortunately, er, it got . . . overlooked until nearly four years later. Such pressure of work'. He pointed at the confusion on his desk. 'I'm afraid that you have no chance of pursuing the claim. My insurers won't let me admit anything but it seems to be my fault . . . I should have issued the writ in time.'

'Who's a clever boy then?' squawked the parrot with remarkable insight.

Mr Ponder was tetchy. 'Can't you control that thing?'

'Nah, leave off! Elvis is all right. So what happens?'

'Well, er Henderson, I can't help you any more. You'll have to consult another solicitor. They may advise you to sue me. I don't know. I'm insured against this sort of thing.' He swallowed hard. The next words were not going to come easily. He felt the General's scornful eyes boring into the back of his balding pate. 'Of course I shan't charge you for what I've done.' He shifted stickily on his chair.

'I should think not,' said Wayne. 'I'd set my heart on buying Blenheim Palace with the damages.' He put another boot on the desk and reclined comfortably. 'A right mess you've made of it. Dad was right. You *are* a berk! So who do I consult?'

'Well, your father consulted Paul Bright.'

'Nah! Not going to Dad's legal eagle.' Perhaps it was the reference to the eagle that did it. Whatever it was, Elvis suddenly took off, flew across the desk and perched on Ponder's shoulder.

'Rumpole, Rumpole of the Bailey,' it squawked into Ponder's whiskery ear.

Ponder's nerves could stand no more. He leapt up and waved a podgy paw to shake off the parrot and was rewarded with a nasty nip on his finger, before Elvis departed with a squawk to the top of the curtain rail.

Ponder wrapped a hanky round his blooded finger and tried to concentrate. 'No. Not Rumpole. He's a barrister. You couldn't consult him. What about Paul Bright's partner? She's got a good reputation. Mary Keen.' He wondered if she was allergic to feathers. 'I think you should go across and see her now.'

'Anything you say chief.' Wayne rose and summoned the parrot which refused to shift. In desperation he and Mr Ponder stood beneath it, trying to coax it down without success. 'It'll just have to stay here until Sharon's back from the Supplementary. She'll get it down, no sweat.'

And then Wayne had gone, leaving Mr Ponder exhausted and nursing his bleeding finger. It had been a long, tiring day.

It wasn't long before Mr Ponder nodded off. Elvis,

a malicious glint in his eye, swooped down and proceeded to shred the last charred remnants of Emily Braithwaite's Last Will and Testament.

The moral of this story is that, while Mr Ponder was correct in saying there is normally a three year time limit it is *not* that simple. In fact, it is rather complex, as we shall see . . .

The
law
of
limitation

In which Wayne learns he has a minor
advantage

Mary Keen, Paul Bright's partner, had always enjoyed a good laugh. She was certainly enjoying one today, as Wayne Henderson had just explained that Mr Ponder had sent him over the road for independent advice, leaving Mr Ponder with a bleeding finger and an errant parrot. 'So let's just recap,' she said. 'Your accident was in October, 1984 and the writ was issued more than three years later. Mr Ponder was quite right. There is a three year rule which means that, normally, claims for personal injury have to be started within three years, but it's not that simple. Parliament has changed the law to make it easier to start proceedings after the three year period. Having said that, those changes aren't going to help you when Mr Ponder had instructions to start proceedings and failed to do so.'

'If I have to sue him. I wouldn't mind. I feel quite narked.'

'Quite so, but there's no need to take it out on my desk,' Mary Keen said dryly. 'Can you please keep your feet on the floor. I do prefer to be able to address you face to face, rather than talking to a pair of size twelves.' She waited for the feet to disappear. 'There's one vital question which I still haven't asked. How old are you?'

'I'm twenty.'

The solicitor started to smile. This quickly turned to a grin. Then she positively hooted with laughter. Wayne wondered what was so funny about being twenty. Nervously he played with the stud in his nose until the laughter died down. 'Come on then, share the joke,' he said.

'It's more ironic than funny. Mr Ponder has sent you away because he thought that he was negligent for not issuing the writ in time.'

'That's right. But you've lost me.'

'You were seventeen when the accident occurred. For people under eighteen, the period for starting proceedings is three years, beginning when they reach the age of eighteen. You have until your twenty-first birthday to issue the writ. So, if you like, you can go back to Mr Ponder. He can carry on with the action.'

It was Wayne's turn to laugh. 'Go back there? The only reason I'm going back there is to pick up the parrot. Look. Maybe I made a big mistake by not coming to see Mr Bright in the first place. It seems that Dad was right. Like, I mean, the Ponderosa's bad news.'

'Mr Ponder is fine,' said Mary Keen defensively, 'so long as he sticks to what he's good at, which isn't litigation. The insurers must have been laughing. He swallowed their limitation point hook, line and sinker.'

'You carry on with my claim, love. You and me get on real fine. What's it worth?'

'I'd need to see all the papers and look at the medical evidence.' Mary Keen was cautious. It was all too easy to give clients an over-optimistic view. 'It must be worth a few bob though. I'll get the legal aid transferred to my firm and have it all sorted out for you.'

Wayne's claim, after transfer of legal aid, was un-eventful. Armed with the medical report and some photographs of Wayne's damaged ear, the insurers paid up within two months. Although they argued that it was partly Wayne's fault, Mary Keen would have none of that and Wayne duly received a cheque for £4,750, plus payment of costs.

Mr Ponder was not very happy about having to remain unpaid for what he had done but things could have been worse. He might have caught psitticosis from the parrot bite.

The rules on time limits are complex and proper advice is essential. The main points are:

- The *basic* rule is a time limit of three years for personal injury claims for all acts of negligence.

- Persons under eighteen (like Wayne) have three years from their eighteenth birthday in which to start proceedings.

- Person of 'unsound mind' have three years from the end of the period of their disability to start proceedings.

- A child suffering ante-natal injuries is deemed to have acquired the injuries at birth, and therefore has eighteen years, plus three years, in which to take proceedings.

- Parliament has given the judges an overriding discretion to ignore the limitation period if it is fair so to do.

- The three year rule can be ignored in cases of fraud, concealment or mistake.

- Normally the three year period runs from the date of the accident, if that is clear-cut. Alternatively, it can run from *the date of knowledge*, where, for example, a person is exposed to an industrial disease but does not know until some time later that he or she has contracted it. The date of knowledge is the date the victim first realised that a significant injury had been suffered; and that the injury was due to an act or omission which is alleged to be negligent or in breach of duty; and the identity of the person to be sued.

Scottish law has developed its own gateways which enable actions to be brought after the three year period in some circumstances.

The
School
Playground

In which Grandma gets a bit of a shock

Grandma Henderson looked at her watch. She'd collected her pension. It was 1.20 p.m. Good, she thought. There was just time to put down a pint of Guinness and be back in the betting shop before the 1.45 at Kempton. She was sure that 'Boneshaker' was going to romp home. She grinned at the prospect, looked both ways and then, holding her umbrella out in front of her like a sword, marched imperiously over the zebra crossing towards the 'Crumb and Crumpet.' An impatient motorcyclist, who skirted round her, had a narrow escape as she retaliated against his impertinence with a vicious jab of the brolly.

The pub was next to the school playground and the noise from the other side of the railings was deafening. Shrieks and shouts of excited children filled the air, so much so that she was drawn to the railings and peered through. About half a dozen boys, out of a class of thirty, aged seven or eight, were chasing round in uncontrolled abandon. 'Get Katie! Get Katie!' came the cry as the youngsters chased the little girl.

Grandma could see at once that the game was out of hand and Katie did not want to be 'got', so much so that she was running in a blind panic, zig-zagging round the playground, frightened and bewildered like a hunted faun.

Grandma was not amused, not least because Katie was her granddaughter. In vain she looked for a teacher to control the position but none was in sight. 'Stop that! Stop that!' cried Grandma but despite the fact that her voice was louder than a regimental sergeant-major's, it was lost in the deafening shouting of the children at play. Thoughts of pints of Guinness forgotten, she entered the playground, brandishing her brolly over her head and ready to clout anyone who was stupid enough to come within range. But she was

171

too late. Even as she advanced, trying to restore some order, she saw Katie take one evasive step too many, trip on a step and fall with a sickening thud against a glass door, which broke with the impact.

The crash of breaking glass and Katie's screams were suddenly the only sound. All the remaining children fell silent in horror at the sight of Katie, head and shoulders through the door, her legs limp.

'Out of the way, you little horrors.' Grandma pushed her way through the frightened children, some of whom had now started to cry as blood began to form in pools on the concrete floor. Feeling faint herself, Grandma gently eased the little girl back, fearful of what she might see. Someone called that a teacher was coming and thirty-five children ran like mad to distance themselves from the incident. Gingerly Grandma pulled Katie back and then lay her on the ground, aghast at the blood flowing from her face and at the distorted position of her right arm, which was obviously broken.

It was at this point that a teacher appeared. 'Get an ambulance at once,' Grandma ordered and the teacher disappeared, returning a few minutes later to confirm that an ambulance was on the way. In the meantime Grandma had been staunching the blood, steeling herself to the sight of the wounds and screams of pain which Katie was still uttering.

The sound of the ambulance siren approaching was like music and, seconds later, Katie was being lifted on to the stretcher. Only then did Grandma weaken. Her legs buckled and her seventy-one year old body slumped to the ground. It was the first time in her life that she had ever fainted.

'Who is she?' asked the ambulanceman but nobody knew and Katie was too badly hurt to tell him.

Grandma gets a bit of a shock

Three weeks later, following a telephone call from Arthur Henderson, Paul Bright called Mary Keen into his office. 'I'd like you to sit in on the next meeting. Katie Henderson has had a serious accident at school. Her father is coming in to give us instructions and I'm so hard pressed at the moment, perhaps you will deal with this claim?'

'Fine by me. Now that I've got Wayne's claim settled, life seems rather dull without a Henderson around. When I gave him his cheque he offered to take me to Skegness for the weekend on his bike.'

'And you accepted of course? I've always said you should settle down.'

Mary was about to retort appropriately when a voice over the intercom announced the arrival of Arthur Henderson and, moments later, he came in, not on his own but with Grandma in hot pursuit. 'Morning Paul, Mary. I don't think you've met my mother—this is Martha Henderson.'

Paul Bright moved round his desk to shake Grandma Henderson's hand but before he got near enough, he was rebuffed. 'I hate solicitors. Just so long as you understand that, we'll get on well. I know you lot. Move at the pace of a snail. Overcharge everyone. Invent difficulties where there are none. Make out wills so complex that we're scared of dying.' With a spindly arm she flourished her brolly which was never far from her right hand, rain or shine. 'I'm only here under sufferance. I want to help Katie. But I've got money on the 1.45 at Plumpton. So don't keep me hanging around.'

Paul Bright was taken aback and Mary also withdrew a pace behind her partner. They had both heard tales from Arthur of Grandma's brushes with an unsuspecting world, but in the flesh she was even more formidable. Standing only five foot three, she had piercing eyes which looked huge behind thick glasses. Her rounded face was wrinkled with seventy-one years of fighting everyone in her path. Dressed as usual in her brown hat, brown tweedy coat, brown brogues and baggy thick-knit stockings which sagged at the knees, her jaw jutted defiantly. The lash of her tongue was known in every shop from one end of the High Street to the other. 'Do sit down Mrs. Henderson. I'm delighted to meet you.' Paul thought that a touch of old fashioned charm would help. 'And I'm sure that you'd like a cup of tea.'

'And you'll put that on the bill and all. No thank you. I know about you lot.' Grandma turned to Mary. 'And who are you? You're the one who actually does the work while Mr Bright here goes off to the golf course every day? Is that right? Tell me I'm right.'

Mary Keen managed a laugh as she retreated behind the desk and sat down beside Paul Bright. 'It's not exactly like that. I'm Paul's partner. We're both here to help young Katie.'

'Doubling the bill, I suppose,' said Grandma.

Beside her, Arthur Henderson shook his head apologetically. The raised eyebrows, the shrug of the shoulders, the resigned look said it all. 'I think we ought to get on with the meeting. We really must help Katie. As I told you over the telephone, she was in the school playground when the children were running riot. We're told there were thirty-seven of them. No one in charge. Six or seven of the younger boys decided to pick on her. What started out as a simple game of chase turned into a frightening experience for her. They were shouting, jeering, all picking on her and threatening to put her head down the loo.'

'That's true. I saw it.' Grandma rapped the desk

with her brolly. 'Like wild animals they were. It was a disgrace. I saw it all. You could see she was terrified and in trying to escape, she missed a step and crashed through a glass door.'

Arthur Henderson was looking to score Brownie points for himself. It would lead to a quiet life at home. 'Mother was wonderful. She was passing by and saw what was going on, hurried into the playground and tried to stop the riot. Unfortunately she didn't get there in time.'

Grandma nodded in agreement. 'What do we pay all our rates and taxes for? Not a teacher in sight.'

Paul Bright thought about it for a moment. 'And Katie had done nothing to provoke this terrorization?'

Arthur was about to say something but was cut dead with the rap of the brolly across his bad knee. He winced as Grandma spoke. 'Of course she didn't. Lovely little girl, our Katie.'

Paul Bright was unhappy about the position and, risking further oral or physical assault, he turned to Arthur. 'But has anyone actually spoken to Katie about what led up to it? From what you told me over the telephone, your mother arrived once the chase had started so she doesn't really know how it all started.' Paul cast a quick look and saw the eyes flashing furiously from behind the thick lenses but Grandma remained silent.

Arthur eased himself further from his mother, distancing himself as far as possible from the danger zone. 'I've spoken to Katie. She didn't provoke anything. And I've asked her whether she's ever been one of the ones to pick on someone else. But she said it's never happened before. Normally the playground is fully supervised and things don't get out of hand.'

'Good, good.' Paul made some notes on his pad.

'And I can count on you, Mrs. Henderson, for a statement, can I? You saw it happen? And you're positive that there was no supervision?'

'Absolutely right. Of course I shall give a statement. I'll give them hell.' For the first time during the meeting her eyes softened and the brolly lay across her lap, rather than clenched in the bird-like white knuckles of her right hand. 'I felt so helpless. I hurried across the playground to where they were chasing Katie. I tried to get them to stop but then she fell. I saw it all. Head first through the glass door, so that she was half one side of it, half the other. There was blood everywhere and her face was something dreadful.'

'Grandma fainted after the ambulance came. She's really not been the same since. It's knocked her sideways,' said Arthur, who was rewarded with a glare which would have melted the Polar Ice Cap. 'If it hadn't been for these pills, I'm sure that she wouldn't have been sleeping at all. Nightmares—the lot.'

Grandma Henderson jutted out her prominent lower jaw. 'Too right. Don't mind blood at all. I dealt with a lot of casualties in the War. Blood doesn't worry me. But what I saw with young Katie . . . that just keeled me over.' It was obvious that Katie was the apple of her eye.

'And how bad is it now?' enquired Paul gently.

'She'll lose the sight of one eye. It's too early to say about the scars but I think they've saved the second eye. The arm is going to be all right. It was a nasty break. Just below the elbow but they tell me it will mend. It's her face that's so sad. She was such a pretty girl.' Arthur's reply was hesitant and heavy with emotion. Slowly he pushed across a picture of a laughing little girl. 'Taken on holiday, this year.'

Paul Bright, seeing that Arthur was close to

breaking point, was quick to intervene. 'We shall pull out all the stops. The law regarding supervision in schools is clear enough. If the playground was un-supervised, then there is a claim for damages alleging negligence. You know well enough by now what I mean by that. Even if there had been *one* teacher on duty for thirty-seven children, it could be argued that that wasn't enough to control these high-spirited children. As it is, from what you've told me, I don't see any defence. Naturally I'd want to hear their point of view before giving a final opinion.'

'Are you doubting what I say?' Grandma had got off her chair and was leaning over the desk.

'No, no, of course not. But I still want to hear what the other side say.'

Mary cut in. 'I agree we shouldn't jump to any conclusions. But this is like another case I handled successfully, where the windows were not toughened. There are British Standards which cover the situation. I think we have a two pronged attack—firstly, lack of supervision and secondly, the inadequacy of the glass.'

'Good point,' agreed Paul, adding 'we will have to show that the lack of supervision caused the accident. We'll need your help on that.' He was looking at Grandma, who had resumed her seat.

'If you mean, could a teacher have prevented it? Then I would say yes. It was obvious what was going on. Clearly, Katie was distressed—she was crying. It took me quite a time to get from outside the railings into the playground. A teacher on the spot would have prevented it.'

'Excellent. And on the question of the glass, I should make clear that breach of British Standards is not enough on its own to establish legal blame, but the standards are good evidence of proper safety levels.

Anthing else you want to add, Mary?'

'There's our old friend, the Occupiers' Liability Act. The school has to be reasonably safe. In deciding what is reasonable, you have to bring into account the age of the people involved. It seems to me that a flimsy door in this type of school is bound to be a breach of the Act.'

'And what about legal aid?' enquired Arthur.

'I'm afraid that your means will be taken into account as Katie is under sixteen. With your damages, unless you've frittered them all, she won't be eligible.'

'I've got an idea.' Mary's face lit up. 'I think Arthur should investigate the cost of plastic surgery and whether Katie would be helped by having it done privately. If so, then I think she should have it and we can claim for the cost of this as part of the damages and, if necessary, obtain an interim payment.'

'Agreed,' replied Paul. 'Arthur, I think you should check whether the NHS can cope with Katie as well as they should. If they can't, then let Mary know and perhaps we could get James McNab, following his success with your wife's operation.'

'He did a wonderful job and I was thinking that perhaps the delays on the National Health Service might mean that Katie would suffer longer than she need. I'll look into it.' Arthur looked pleased 'What about Katie tripping over a step?' Can't it be said the accident was her own fault?'

'I doubt it. It could mean, in some cases, that she'd not kept a proper look out, but not here. She's under ten and Judges are reluctant to hold children blame-worthy. Their conduct is judged in comparison with other children of the same age. Anyway, the step itself, close to a door, could be an example of unsafe design of premises—a further point against the local authority.'

Paul paused and smiled at Grandma. 'Turning to you, I'd say you've got a claim worth pursuing for damages for nervous shock. It's clear, from what you said, that not only were you there when it happened, but also you saw the nastiness of it all and it has knocked you sideways ever since.'

Grandma Henderson smiled. Arthur was shocked at this strange phenomenon. 'Me? Got a claim? You'd better pursue it.'

'We'll get a statement from your doctor about your health. Armed with that, I think we can succeed.'

Some hazards of life

A witness to a gruesome incident of any kind who does suffer ill health (as opposed to mere passing distress), as a result of what was seen, does have a claim for compensation. Furthermore, someone who was not a witness can, if the circumstances are convincing, get damages for nervous shock on learning of a nasty accident happening to a loved one. Again, there has to be more than passing grief before this claim can be entertained. Such claims arise against the person who caused the injury to the loved one, but only if that person was negligent.

A child can be held to blame, wholly or partly, if he or she was not as careful as other children of that age would be. A child of fifteen has been found to blame (ie negligent) for pushing someone into a swimming pool. Whether the victim can actually get the damages paid turns on whether the child was insured through a parent, or has funds to pay. A parent is not *automatically* liable for negligent acts of a child. It depends on whether the parent was negligent in permitting the situation to arise—for example, a parent who supplies a seven year old child with a flick knife could be sued for negligence if that child carelessly or deliberately injured someone.

A school is not automatically liable if one child assaults another. It depends on the particular circumstances.

Children are likely to trespass, that is, go onto other people's land without consent. If an injury is sustained, then a claim may still arise, depending on the circumstances. The 'occupier' of the land within the legal meaning can be liable to a child if he knew of the child's presence or knew of facts from which a reasonable person would assume that trespass was likely. A classic example is a public footpath across a railway line where the stile is not in place, so that it is easy for children to play on the track. British Rail has been held responsible in such a situation. Building sites are another attraction to children and similar liabilities can arise against the person responsible.

Katie's accident occurred primarily from lack of supervision, with the injuries being sustained because of the unsafe premises. A step, whilst harmless enough in many situations, may be a danger either because it is in such a position that it is not obvious, or because experience has shown that people, for some reason, do repeatedly fall.

Dangerous storage of inflammables can give rise to liability. So can icy playgrounds or slippery floors. The facts need to be carefully checked. For example, slipping on spilt food in the school or factory canteen, or in a restaurant, may give rise to no claim at all. It depends whether there was a safe system for keeping the floor reasonably clean. An isolated lump of mashed potato, which may have fallen only seconds before someone else treads on it, is unlikely to give rise to a successful claim. But if the system for clearing plates is so haphazard that garbage is repeatedly falling on to the floor, then liability may well arise.

Falls in supermarkets are common because customers slip on items knocked over by other customers. Successful claims are possible but not easy. It is necessary to show that the supermarket had an unsafe system of stacking goods or of checking to make sure that spillages were rapidly cleared up.

A child taking part in school games is taken to have accepted the risks inherent in playing that game. Most sporting accidents, and other accidents at school, are sheer bad luck, and because there is no negligence on the part of the school, the school will not be liable. For this reason, parents should consider insurance to cover accidents at school.

For example, suppose a child fractures his spine playing rugby and is paralysed. If there were negligence on the part of the school, then damages could be as high as £500,000. Proving negligence is difficult, but an accident insurance policy taken out by the parent would provide a substantial sum, which could be invaluable in safeguarding the child's future.

If, however, a sports injury is sustained because the game has got out of hand because of lack of supervision by a suitably qualified member of staff, the school may be held responsible. Likewise if the pitch is unsafe—for example, a rock hard rugby pitch, or if there is insufficient coaching.

If a player is injured, for example, in a game of hockey, by a deliberate and unprovoked attack with a hockey stick, then the other player is responsible for damages *for assault*. Negligence is not relevant to this unless the game was not being adequately controlled or if the players had not been adequately taught the rules of the game. The parent of an aggressor child who had carried out the assault would not normally be liable.

Katie's claim

In which Grandma smiles for a second time

Mary Keen stood in the court corridor, waiting to see the Master who had been assigned to approve the settlement of Katie's claim. David Appleby, solicitor for the insurers, was sitting on a bench a few feet away, having a last minute look at his notes. There was no tension in the air. Terms had been agreed between them and it was merely a matter of getting the Master to rubber stamp them. 'It's 2.15. Shall we go in?' enquired Mary of her opponent, who immediately rose to his feet as he nodded his assent. Mary knocked on the large wooden door and was beckoned in, followed by Arthur Henderson and Katie, with David Appleby bringing up the rear.

'Good afternoon,' said the Master, who was sitting behind a large wooden desk, in a lofty, rather charmless room deep in the heart of the Law Courts in the Strand. 'Do sit down.' He smiled at Arthur, who was holding his daughter's hand. 'I suggest that you sit at the end there.' He pointed to a pair of chairs in the line in front of his desk.

'Good afternoon Master. If it please you, my name is Mary Keen and I am the solicitor acting on behalf of Mr Henderson who is the next friend for his daughter Katie. My friend Mr Appleby appears on behalf of the school. I'm sure that you will have read the pleadings and you will be aware of Katie's nasty injuries from an accident at school, some two and a half years ago. There's been no delay in pursuing the claim but it has taken this length of time for the medical consultants to form a view about the future effect of the injuries upon her.'

The Master, who was dressed in a black jacket and pin-stripe trousers, with a white shirt and sober blue tie, nodded his head in agreement. 'Yes. I see that the school did deny liability in their defence but the settlement is on a full liability basis? No contributory negligence on the part of Katie? Is that right?'

David Appleby was quick to agree. 'Yes Master. Despite the terms of the defence, without prejudice negotiations between myself and Miss Keen have led to a situation where an offer was made, which she was able to recommend to her client, not just based on her own experience but, in this matter, supported by advice from counsel.'

'I think I should see counsel's advice.'

'Here it is, Master,' said Mary Keen. 'As you will see, it is from Mr Jeremy Sprigg who is very experienced in these matters. Master, in many cases, I do not bring the plaintiff to court for approval of damages but, as this is a disfigurement case, I though it would help you to see Katie for yourself, before making up your mind whether this is an appropriate settlement.'

'I always think that's a good idea. Now I'll just study Mr Sprigg's views.' For a few moments the Master was silent, as he read the advice. Then he studied the medical reports and the photographs of what the injuries had looked like, before lastly asking Katie to come forward to sit in front of him. The Master, who was himself a trained barrister of many years experience before accepting his present post, had a kindly face and Katie cheerfully chatted to him about school and what she wanted to do when she grew up. As she was chatting, the Master was forming his own view of the blemishes left on her face.

Jeremy Sprigg had valued the claim for pain and suffering and loss of amenity at £24,000 for the loss of the eye, the scars—which had nearly gone, following surgery—and for the broken arm. 'And I understand, Miss Keen, that you have negotiated a settlement for £24,000, plus £1,250 for interest on general damages.'

'Yes Master. Additionally there were special damages for travelling and ruined clothing. The cost of plastic surgery was agreed by my friend's clients, who paid for the cost as an interim payment. The only outstanding specials total £1,450, including interest.

'What about the future? In this sort of case I'm regularly hearing suggestions that the child would have been Miss United Kingdom or would have been an airline stewardess. Is this an issue?' This was the voice of the cynic who had seen so many claims put forward on the most wildly optimistic basis.

Mary laughed. 'No Master. Katie says that she has always wanted to work with handicapped people. The loss of her eye will not make a difference. Nevertheless, on the basis that things can change, I have negotiated the sum of £2,500 because she is not as free in her choice of jobs and might end up worse off. Counsel considers the figure fair but there is no claim for future loss of earnings as such. There is a claim for the further cost of optical treatment and replacement of her artificial eye from time to time. Based on the medical evidence, this has been calculated, and I am seeking your approval for an agreed further sum of £7,500. This gives a final total claim of £36,700, excluding the interim payment.'

The Master jotted on a piece of paper for a moment. 'I am very happy to approve this settlement. It seems fair in the circumstances and I make an order by consent; the defendants to pay the plaintiff's costs to be taxed.' He turned to Katie. 'This is a great deal of money and will be invested for you by the court and you will be entitled to this money when you are eighteen. I am now going to release the amount which your father paid for travelling expenses and so on.' He smiled at her. 'Further, I propose releasing another

186

£350 so that you can buy something useful or have a holiday. The rest must, however, remain in court for the time being. Although you have been through a most horrible accident, I am sure you will be a great success in life and you remain, if I may say so, a most highly attractive young girl.'

There was a shuffling of chairs and Mary Keen led everyone from the room, Katie still blushing furiously.

'Goodbye then,' said David Appleby. 'I'll make arrangements for the funds to be paid into court.'

'Thank you.' Mary then led her clients down the gloomy passages, before crossing the Strand and entering the café opposite. They self-served themselves to tea and buns and waited for Grandma's appearance. It wasn't long before she arrived, brown hat at a jaunty angle and with a positive spring in her step. With a few jabs and parries of her brolly, she pushed her way to the front of the queue, got herself a cup of tea before the dozen people who had been waiting, and then joined the three of them sitting at the table.

Without waiting to find out how Katie got on, Grandma opened her bag and produced a betting slip. 'While I was hanging around, waiting for you, I decided to invest my damages for nervous shock on a horse called "Law's Delays".'

'What!' said Arthur. 'The whole lot?'

'Well . . .' Grandma said, slightly defensively, 'I did have the odd pint of Guinness at lunch.' She licked her lips in remembrance. 'So I put £3,250 to win on this outsider. It seemed like an omen.' She flourished the betting slip again. 'And it won. Romped home.'

'So how much did you win?' asked Arthur.

'I shall clear over £70,000. The bookies have sent out for more cash. I've decided to buy myself a new car. I'm tired of the old Morris Minor.' She sipped her tea loudly. 'I think I'll take back what I said about solicitors. You've done well. I'll send you a crate of Guinness.'

Children and persons of unsound mind cannot run litigation in their own name. Normally a parent or close relatives acts as 'next friend', standing in their shoes. Sometimes a solicitor is appointed as next friend if there is conflict of interest between parent and child. The court also has power to make an appointment. For these purposes, 'children' means those under eighteen in England and Wales; or, in Scotland, boys under fourteen and girls under twelve.

Compensation claims which do not go to court, and most do not, are settled by negotiation between the parties. No approval of the settlement is usually necessary. However, for children under the age of eighteen and for persons of unsound mind, the terms are generally approved by the court. Normally this is by a Master or, out of London, by a District Registrar of the High Court, but the approval can be given by a judge.

For obvious reasons, someone under eighteen or of unsound mind is not permitted to control substantial damages. The funds are normally invested by the court, but sums can be released for good reasons.

The
pills
that
went
wrong

In which Arthur suffers the flat cap
syndrome

Paul Bright looked at his diary and saw that Arthur Henderson was due to come in at 11.15. His secretary told him that Arthur had refused to give a reason. Most unusual.

At 11.15 precisely, Arthur was shown in and, although it was a warm May morning, he was wearing a big flat cap and a gloomy look. 'Do sit down Arthur. I'm glad to see you.'

'And you, but I'm sorry to say that I've got another problem.'

'Not another road accident, is it?'

'No. Yet it's connected with it in a way. The medics have always said that I'd suffer increasing pain from arthritis in my knee. Well, needless to say, they were right, so I saw my G.P. He sent me to the specialist who was reluctant to operate unless I found the pain unbearable. It wasn't quite that bad.'

Paul Bright then realised why his client had consulted him but he thought it better to let Arthur get there in his own words.

'So what happened next?'

'I was taking some arthritis pills till Christmas 1987.' He looked crestfallen, ashamed of what he was about to reveal but then suddenly he took his courage and his flat cap in both hands and, with a swift movement, pulled it off to reveal that he was now completely bald. Where, only weeks before, there had been a full head of hair, wiry, springy, unruly and rarely flattened for long, even by the most generous dosage of water, there was now nothing. Hurriedly Arthur put his cap back on.

'I'm sorry. What a dreadul thing to happen but I'd guessed as much. You're a victim of what's now known as the 'Flat Cap Syndrome.' I was reading an article about it in the Law Gazette. There's any number of solicitors who have been consulted by people like yourself, men and women, all of whom have gone completely bald after taking these pills. Some have also got other skin troubles and internal problems as well. Have you got anything like that?'

'No. Thankfully not. Not so far anyway.'

'Yes. They took it off the market after the Committee on Safety of Medicines intervened. It is suggested that the drug was inadequately researched, its beneficial effects exaggerated, its side effects suppressed and its period on the market too long before it was withdrawn.'

'You seem to know more about it than me. So what am I going to do?'

'Firstly you're not going to spend all your damages on litigation. Can you imagine what it will cost to take on a major drug company? Without legal aid, your damages would soon be spent. I don't want to see Arthur Henderson carrying the banner at the head of a queue of all the litigants. After all, I might have to advise you that there was insufficient evidence to prove negligence.'

'Oh! We're back to negligence, are we. No blame—no claim.'

'Yes. The new law doesn't apply to you I'm afraid. There was no contract between yourself and the drug company. From what you've told me, I don't think that your GP was negligent in prescribing this particular pill. He took you off them last Christmas at the same time as everyone else. So the claim would primarily be against the drug company and possibly also against the licensing ministers and against the Committee on Safety of Medicines. They are responsible for approval of the sale of the drug on the UK market and monitor its subsequent progress, but I'm not saying that they *are* to blame!'

'It seems most unfair to me that I should have to prove negligence when it's quite obvious that I and lots of others like me are going round in flat caps due to taking this drug. Why can't they just pay up?'

'They might do. Other drug companies have formed schemes for payment of compensation without admitting any blame. There was the Eraldin drug and of course Thalidomide, where proper compensation was produced. Other drug companies have taken the view that litigants must prove their case and in consequence have ground down a large number of people who could not afford to litigate.'

'And you're telling me that I can't afford to litigate. I don't feel like giving up. What should I do?'

'I'm afraid that the law is in a real mess at the moment. In the USA you can run a 'class action' where a test case or cases are brought on behalf of a large number of people. When the outcome of the class action is known, all the claims are settled on that basis. The English courts do not recognise that concept. You may remember another arthritis drug called Opren where there has been a considerable fuss, and an eventual offer of settlement. A group of experienced solicitors got together and formed a committee to help a vast number of people who had allegedly suffered from taking that drug. They then started some test cases on legal aid, but the courts decided that in selecting which cases to take to court, it was not possible to choose cases with legally aided claimants only, when there was a vast body of other litigants who, in theory, were well enough off to fight the case. The court then decided that the legally aided cases could proceed, so long as the non-legally aided litigants paid their share.'

Arthur thought about it for a moment. 'That seems fair.'

'Fair it may be but impractical is the word I'd use, with costs running into millions. In your case I don't know what damages the court would award for total baldness. Even if we assume £5,000, or even £10,000, it would still be a drop in the ocean compared with the share of the costs which you would have to stake to win even that sum. It's not an attractive proposition. Not even for a gambler like your mother.'

'So what now?'

'Well, the Master of the Rolls, who's a top judge, realised that there was an injustice and has urged that there should be law reform. Possibly there *will* be recognition of the class action type of claim, or, I hope, some amendment to the legal aid rules.'

'But what now then?' Arthur unthinkingly pulled the cap more firmly down towards his ears.

'I think it's worth getting you involved with any bandwaggon which is rolling in the hope that we can shame the drug company by public exposure and legal argument into creating a tariff scheme to pay compensation without admitting anything.'

'Doesn't the new law help me?'

'No. You took your pills under the old law, so that negligence has to be proved. Even so, the new law is not as magic as you might expect. The Consumer Protection Act 1987 introduced strict liability to replace negligence. In theory this places a far greater responsibility on manufacturers of all sorts of products —including drugs. But the problem is that the new law also provides a big escape route—the 'development risks' defence. Companies will still be able to argue that no one could reasonably have expected the consequences which developed from their drug. If they can prove that, then they escape liability. Obviously they will have to show that they undertook all the proper tests and so on, but nevertheless, the new Act doesn't give the consumer nearly so much protection because of this let-out.'

'Nothing is ever as easy as it seems,' said Arthur gloomily. 'Looks as if I shall have to buy a wig.'

'Or learn to live with your baldness. You might be interested to know that another drug, being tested to cure an internal complaint, turned out to have the side effect of making hair grow and is becoming available here. It's already on sale in some countries. Have a word with your doctor about that.'

'But, in the meantime then?'

'It's toe-dipping time only. If we can join with a large number of others, then it's worth seeing what develops.'

'I'm prepared to put up to £3,500.'

'Leave it with me. I'll see you again when I've made some more investigations.'

Strength
in
numbers

In which Arthur gets a hair deal

Paul Bright's brow furrowed. His receptionist had just told him that Arthur Henderson had arrived. Nothing unusual in that but there was just something odd about her voice, as if she were trying to give him a message. Odd, he decided as he arranged Arthur's papers on his desk and then went to meet his client. It had been some months since they had met, months in which the solicitor had made considerable progress. He swung open the door into reception. There were four or five clients sitting around the room, gazing at the technology, looking at magazines or staring into space. He looked round. Funny. Where's Arthur? He turned to Mandy, who was sitting at her word processor with a smirk on her face. 'Where's Mr Henderson?' he said.

Before Mandy could answer, a voice from behind him spoke. 'Here I am.' The solicitor spun round at the familiar voice. 'Didn't you recognise me?' said Arthur.

'Sorry, I must have missed you behind your newspaper,' said the solicitor, hastily covering his confusion. 'Let's go through.'

Settled comfortably in Paul's office, it was Arthur who spoke first. 'What do you think of it then? Cost me an arm and a leg.' The solicitor swallowed hard and looked at the wig again. Arthur had a head of the most luxurious black hair.

'It . . . er . . . makes you look so much younger, a great improvement on the baldness.'

Arthur beamed with pride. 'Elizabeth Taylor was right. The funny thing is that if you know that you look good, you feel good. It's taken years off me.'

'It's a great improvement,' Paul repeated, thinking of nothing better to say. 'Anyway, the good news is that you've been lucky. Strength in numbers. That's what counted. A group of solicitors did get together, a committee was formed and I was on it. We've had meetings with the DHSS and with lawyers representing the company and have been pooling all the evidence from various sources. That evidence shows that the company should have withdrawn the drug from the market a long time ago, even assuming that it was proper that it got offered for sale at all. The company misled the Committee on Safety of Medicines right to the end. We were helped because a 'mole' from the company sent copies of confidential in-house tests on the drug to the Committee on Safety of Medicines and to us. The company has now admitted the authenticity of the documents and, as it is self-evident that the company will be found liable for negligence under the old law, they first offered 90% but we've negotiated now for 100% of proper losses, plus costs.

'How much will I get?'

'Your only adverse effect was hair fall-out. The company are saying that, if you went to court, the full value for total baldness, for someone with a good head of hair, would be £8,000. There will also be your special damages for out of pocket expenses, but not the cost of the wig. They say that the damages are ample for you to suffer baldness or buy a wig. They've got a point. How much did it cost?'

'I've got the receipt. It wasn't cheap but it was worth every penny of it. £1,200, plus VAT. But I'll settle for £8,000 all up, plus costs.'

'I'll set it up. You'll be glad to know that the drug company are not seeking to offset the saving in expense of hair cuts.' Paul Bright grinned. 'On that basis, I'd say the deal's a snip.'

Claims for damages for unexpected side effects of drugs are notoriously difficult—not just from the point of view of proving the manufacturer is responsible, but also because of the problems of financing these long and complex claims. As Paul Bright said, it is not clear how much difference the new law—The Consumer Protection Act 1987—will make. As finally passed by Parliament, the Act is not nearly as strong as it might have been. The most fruitful claims against drug companies have succeeded largely because of a blaze of publicity generated by the victims, their families, solicitors and other sympathisers.

Susie
and
the
dog

In which Arthur has animal instincts

It was a fine summer evening and Paul Bright was sitting in his garden, enjoying a glass of beer. All round him the flowers were in bloom, the birdsong was a joy and he felt at peace with the world after a long day with clients' problems. He looked at his watch. Time for another beer and then the News and Test Match Special. He rose from the patio and was heading for the fridge and a chilled lager when the telephone rang. 'Paul Bright here,' he responded.

'I'm sorry to trouble you at home. I hope you don't mind.' It was Arthur Henderson. 'I just had to talk to somebody. I'm phoning from the hospital. Susie, that's my youngest, has just been admitted. She was savaged by a dog in the park this evening. She's in intensive care. We're all down here. I just felt that, as you'd seen us through so many different problems, it would help to talk to you.'

'I'll come straight over.'

'No. I didn't mean that. There's no need for you to spoil your evening.'

'Of course I'll come. Give me ten minutes.' He put down the phone, cast a wistful glance at the fridge and, pausing only to put on a jacket, was quickly into his Audi and on the way.

He found Ward 6b without difficulty and, in the waiting room, saw the massed ranks of the Henderson family standing in an anxious group, Arthur in his wig, Jackie with the successful facelift behind her, Grandma still flourishing her umbrella and Wayne reading a pop magazine, apparently without a care in the world. Katie, looking frightened, sat silently on a bench.

Grandma Henderson saw him first and flourished her brolly in his direction. 'Wake up Arthur. Mr Bright's here.' Everyone turned to face him and, after brief pleasantries, the solicitor took Arthur and his wife down the green linoleum of the corridor to where they could talk privately in an empty day-room. Arthur explained the situation. 'Susie's only six. She was playing in the park with a friend before going to bed. They were throwing a tennis ball around when this Alsatian came bounding up and started to guard the ball. Susie's little friend, Alison, was frightened and ran away, but Susie's always liked dogs and, although it was growling, she went to pick up the ball. The dog flew at her, grabbing her by the throat and pinning her to the ground.'

'How do you know all this—were you there?'

'No, the children were on their own but there were plenty of people about. The owner of the Alsatian was apparently two or three hundred yards away, sitting on a seat, according to this nice young couple who just happened to be close by. They saw everything. They heard the dog growling and shouted a warning to Susie but she either didn't hear or didn't care. Anyway it was them, or rather him, who grabbed a litter bin and very bravely hit the dog over the head with it several times, until it let go. By then the owner was coming across, having heard the noise, and he called the dog to heel.'

'So poor little Susie lost a lot of blood, did she?'

'Yes. She was badly bitten, but this woman used her own clothing to staunch the blood, and they carried Susie to the car and took her to the hospital. She was here in less than two minutes. If it had been further, I think she would have been dead already,' added Arthur.

Jackie Henderson clung to her husband. 'She's going to be all right, isn't she?'

Arthur put his arm round her, 'Yes dear,' but Paul Bright knew from Arthur's face that he too was very worried. All the awesome possibilities went through Paul's mind—brain damage, scarring, speech defects or, worse still, death. The thought chilled him, not least the legal implications if death were to follow: trivial damages for a start—always a hard thing to explain to distraught parents.

'Come on,' Paul said. 'I'm sure someone will find a cup of tea for both of you to help while away the time. Did they say how long it would be before the crisis would be over?'

'No.'

'I'll stay anyway, as long as you want.' He followed them back down the corridor and they sent Wayne off to fetch tea, Grandma spurring him into action with a barbed remark and an even more pointed prod of the umbrella.

'Where's the dog owner?' asked Paul.

'Well might you ask. He disappeared. But this couple, the Franklins, who brought Susie in, said they'd know him again. They're keen to find him because the owner was very unpleasant. Said that Susie had been provoking the dog and, thinking that this chap Franklin was Susie's father, told him off for hitting his dog.'

Paul Bright said nothing, but felt that warning flags were being hoisted. 'I'm going to phone the police. From what you've told me, this dog is a menace to the community. I'll ring them now. Perhaps when I get back there'll be some good news about Susie.'

'The police think they know the owner. Of course they knew nothing about it because there was no 999 call, with the Franklins taking Susie to the hospital. But luckily the desk sergeant was able to have a word with one or two of the bobbies on the beat and they knew a man who regularly takes his Alsatian into the park.

Then, hopefully, the Franklins will be able to identify him.' He was about to continue when a young doctor in a white coat, hands deep in pockets, stethoscope swaying as he walked, came through the swing doors towards them. Arthur thought the look on his face suggested that devastating news was at hand, but it was only the long hours which had drained him. 'I've good news. She's pulled through the last hour. That was the crisis. What's more, we think that the prompt action of the people who brought her in saved her. If that man hadn't got the dog off when he did, I'm afraid you'd have lost her. Have you found the owner yet?'

'No.' It was Paul Bright who shook his head. 'The police are working on it.'

'It'll have to be put down, that's my view,' said the doctor.

'And the owner too,' said Arthur angrily, thinking of what the Franklins had told him about the owner's attitude. 'Let's start with him.'

'I know how you feel, Arthur, but let's just be thankful that Susie has been saved! Leave it to me to sort out the legalities.'

'Should be strung up,' said Grandma. 'Just wait till I get my hands on that man. And his dog.'

Paul Bright decided it was time to leave. It had been a long day.

Back home he poured himself a lager and switched on the television in time to see Richie Benaud bidding viewers goodnight from Lords after what he called 'the most exciting day's cricket in years.'

203

Animals—
wild
or
tame

In which Arthur learns the meaning of
danger

'I'm so pleased that Susie is doing well,' said Paul Bright. 'I've spoken to the consultant and he's told me just what a close thing it was.'

Arthur pushed back the fringe of his wig, in a mannerism which had become all too familiar to those who knew him. 'We were so lucky and I'm delighted the police were able to prosecute the owner.'

'I had no sympathy for him,' agreed Paul. 'I did have some sympathy for the dog—did you know it was called Jaws? The magistrates made the right decision ordering that the dog be destroyed. It seems sad in a way but really the evidence at the magistrates' court was overwhelming—this was an unprovoked attack and plainly it was the type of thing which could happen again to any other child. The magistrates had the alternative power, having decided that the dog was dangerous, to order that the owner should keep the dog under proper control. But the owner was his own worst enemy telling the magistrates he had no intention of keeping the dog on a lead in public, and generally appearing unrepentant.'

'I suppose that means that a claim for damages by Susie is home and dry?'

Paul Bright shook his head. 'I'm sorry, not at all.' Yet as he spoke, there was a knowing look on his face which Arthur could not understand.

Arthur was indignant. 'Why? The magistrates have found the dog was dangerous. The owner or his insurers, if he has them, must pay up.'

'That's not the law, although a lot of people think it is. The magistrates, having decided that the dog was dangerous, can make an order for it to be destroyed. It doesn't have to be proved that the owner *knew* the dog was dangerous. Because the dog behaved in an unprovoked and dangerous way with Susie, that was enough for the magistrates not to take the risk of exposing the public to the possibility of a further attack.'

Arthur was furious. 'So you mean that, because the owner told the magistrates that the dog had never attacked before, he can get away with it? That Susie's scarring will go uncompensated?' His eyes flashed angrily.

'I'm sorry Arthur, but entirely different laws apply when seeking compensation for injuries caused by animals. For an attack by a dog, you have to show that the owner *knew* that the dog was likely to be dangerous.'

'Is that what Parliament has laid down? *They* ought to be shot. There's my little Susie, with scarring all round her neck, broken ribs, and you tell me that Parliament leaves her without any remedy. It's a scandal.'

'Just calm down Arthur,' said Paul soothingly. 'I didn't say that.'

'Sorry,' said Arthur. 'It's just when I think of Susie lying there in the park, being savaged by a dog, it seems so wrong that she might not be compensated. She's still having nightmares now.'

'Of course. I understand. What Parliament laid down in the Animals Act was that, if an animal belongs to a *dangerous species*, then the keeper of the animal is strictly liable. So, if you keep your pet cobra in the cocktail cabinet and it escapes and bites Grandma, you don't have to prove negligence.'

Arthur laughed. 'I'd put it the other way round. It's more likely that Grandma would attack the cobra. Perhaps I need a licence for her?'

'You're not going to draw me on the behaviour of one of my favourite clients,' said Paul with an impish grin. 'In the case of a dog, or an animal which is not regarded as dangerous, such as a horse, the keeper is strictly liable in two situations. First, where the injury is of the kind which the animal (unless restrained) is likely to cause; or, second, if the injury was likely to be severe and . . .'

'We can show that,' interjected Arthur.

'Hold on! There's more yet. With animals like horses or dogs, you have to prove that the likelihood of severe injury was due to characterisitics of *that animal* not normally found in animals of the same species. Put simply and worst of all, you have to show that these characteristics were known to the owner.'

'I see.' Arthur had grasped the difficulty.

'The answer is to show that Jaws was known to the owner to be likely to bite humans. It is not sufficient, for example, just to show a tendency to bite other animals.'

Arthur looked depressed again. 'We're stuck then. The owner says that the dog had never attacked anyone.'

'Well I for one don't necessarily accept what he says as right. After all, we know from the Franklins that his immediate attitude at the time of the attack was to blame Susie. The magistrates would have none of that nonsense.'

'So how do we prove a case?'

'You obviously weren't listening to local radio this morning. I put out an appeal for anyone who had ever been bitten or terrified by an Alsatian down in the park to come forward. We've had three telephone calls already.'

'You've certainly built up the suspense,' chided Arthur. 'Now you tell me. I thought you were winding me up.'

'Always was a bit of a dark horse, if that's the right

analogy,' said Paul. 'One caller told me about an incident about twenty-five years ago. That's hopeless. The other two were quite recent, where an Alsatian called Jaws, without any provocation, pushed over a young child and was called off by the owner as it was about to bite and, in the other incident, an old dear sitting on a seat had the sleeve of her coat ripped when a dog called Jaws sprang at her.'

'Splendid. So we're home and dry then?'

'It looks as if we can prove that the owner knew about Jaws' dangerous instincts. If the owner had taken heed of the two previous incidents, Susie would never have been attacked.'

'Just suppose,' said Arthur slowly 'that Susie had died. I know, from all your other advice about damages for personal injury. But what about if she had died? What then?'

'Rightly or wrongly, Parliament has decreed that, for the death of children, the damages should be £3,500, which many parents regard as trivial or even obscene. Remember the Zeebrugge disaster? The solicitors acting there were able to negotiate with the shipping company for damages far in excess of the amount laid down by Parliament and obtained offers of £10,000 for the death of a child. Nevertheless, some parents were outraged even at this offer, which I can understand, but damages are not intended to be a form of punishment. They are designed to provide compensation, so far as money can compensate, and the view of Parliament was that such a tragic loss cannot be measured in cash, so they pitched the figure low.'

Arthur gave a low whistle. 'I never knew that. Is there anything else we need to sort out?'

'No. I'm seeing these witnesses and then we'll set about getting the money out of Jaws' keeper. By the way, I've also been consulted by the parents of Susie's friend, Alison. She too is still suffering nightmares from seeing the attack, even although she had run off. You've no objection if I pursue a claim for her as well?'

'No. She must have been terrified. You do everything you can for her.'

'Everything else all right at home? I'm planning an early retirement on all the money I'm making out of your family.'

'Touch wood, everything's fine at the moment. Mind you, you might be hearing from Mother sometime. You remember she won over £70,000 on that horse, 'Law's Delays'? Well anyway, she's bought a red Ferrari. She's the scourge of south London.'

'I'll watch out for her.'

The lawyers' zoo

As Paul Bright explained, the Animals Act, which applies to England and Wales, makes the 'keeper' (usually the owner) of an animal strictly liable for injury caused by the animal, so that it is not necessary to prove negligence in order to win compensation. However, if the animal is of a non-dangerous species, for example, a cat, dog, horse, cow, goat, sheep, (believe it or not) a bull, or a stick insect, the owner will not be liable unless it can be proved that he or she *knew* the animal had dangerous characteristics. On the other hand, there is no need to prove the owner knew the animal was dangerous if it belongs to a dangerous species—lions, tigers, bears, elephants, some monkeys and crocodiles fall into this group.

The ordinary rules of negligence still apply as well. For example, if the owner of a dog lets it roam freely on the road, causing a car to swerve and injure the occupants, the dog owner can be sued for negligence, because a duty of care is owed to road users.

In Scotland, the usual rules of negligence also apply, but there is a completely different Act of Parliament, called, not surprisingly, the Animals (Scotland) Act, which takes a somewhat different approach to the question of strict liability.

Fatal accidents

As Paul Bright explained, the death of a child under eighteen does not give rise to a large claim for damages. The figure laid down by Parliament is currently £3,500. This can be changed from time to time, and since the present limit has been in force since 1982, it is time for it to be raised. Where the damages are awarded to both parents, the sum of £3,500 is divided between them.

If the deceased person was under eighteen and had never married, the parents may make this claim for bereavement. If the child was illegitimate, however, only the mother can claim. Otherwise, a claim for damages for bereavement can be made only by the husband or wife of the person who died.

Large claims arising from death occur when there are surviving persons—dependants of the deceased. Thus, for example, the death of an adult child who had been providing his parents with financial support could give rise to a claim by the parents, not for the sum of £3,500 for bereavement, but instead for the loss of their income from their child, if it can be proved that the payments would have continued.

In such cases, compensation is based on putting the dependants back in the same position, financially, as if the death had not occurred. No damages are awarded for grief, although in some circumstances there could be a claim for nervous shock (see page 180).

Dependants who can claim in a fatal accident case include:

- the wife or husband, or former wife or husband, of the deceased;

- someone who has been living with the deceased as wife or husband for at least two years;

- a parent or grandparent;

- a child or grandchild;

- a person who, although not the deceased's own child, was treated as a child of the deceased, for example, a spouse's child by a previous marriage;

- a sister, brother, uncle or aunt, or their issue.

The action is usually begun by the executors or administrators of the deceased's estate, but in some circumstances it may be brought by the claimants themselves.

In assessing the damages, the court looks at the financial effect of the death on each dependant. The court may not take into account the remarriage, or prospects of remarriage, of the widow(er). This used to be an awkward and embarrassing point until the law was changed. Where the claimant is a common law spouse, the court must take this into account, inevitably by way of reducing the award, since the claimant has no *enforceable* right to financial support. The court must disregard any benefits which come to the claimant from the estate—such as gifts under the Will.

By way of example, suppose that Arthur had been killed in his accident. His executors (if he had made a Will) or his administrators (if he had not) would take proceedings on behalf of his dependants. These could be Jackie, the children (not necessarily Wayne) and Grandma if she were financially dependent on Arthur, her son. The damages would be calculated by reference to:

- Arthur's age;
- his income and the number of years he would have been expected to earn it; and
- how long the various dependants would, in fact, have been financially dependent on Arthur;

A reduction would be made from Arthur's income to allow for the fact that part of it was used to support himself. The value of any jobs which Arthur did around the house, such as car maintenance, gardening and decorating, which Jackie would now have to pay someone else to do, could be the subject of an additional claim.

Remember that damages are to provide compensation, not to punish the wrong-doer.

The
Ferrari
and
the
crushing
blow

In which Grandma has a different kind of
windfall

Paul Bright looked out of his office window. It was a fine, clear morning and promised to be the first perfect day of the summer. Pity to be shut in an office, he decided as he stretched over to pick up the telephone which was urgently buzzing beside him.

'Yes?'

Jane, the new receptionist who had only started the previous week, sounded shell-shocked, her voice quiet but quivering. 'There's a client to see you. She hasn't got an appointment. She says that you'll see her anyway. It's Mrs Martha Henderson.'

Bright groaned. 'I'm in the middle of getting some urgent papers off to counsel. You know I'd set aside the morning. Can you ask her to come back after lunch, or perhaps she could see someone else?'

He paused and heard Jane passing on the message to Mrs Henderson. Then the familiar rasp of Grandma's voice came clearly down the line. 'Of course he'll see me. It's most important.'

'OK Jane. I heard that. I'm coming through.' With a sigh, he bundled up the two feet high stack of papers which had to be in the Temple by three o'clock. Bang goes lunch in the pub garden. It'll be a sandwich at the desk, he decided, a thought which irritated him as he paced resignedly through to the waiting room. But the smile on his face as he saw Mrs Martha Henderson told nothing of his innermost thoughts. 'How nice to see you, Mrs Henderson. I gather you want to talk to me urgently.'

The small, wiry figure advanced towards him with brisk steps. Behind the glasses, the small eyes glowered, her every movement bristling with indignation. Though the temperature outside was pushing into the eighties, she was still dressed in her sensible brown shoes, thick stockings, tweedy coat and brown hat. 'At once, at once.'

No sooner had she sat down in his office than she jumped up again, delving deep into her pocket. 'Look at this, take a look at this.' She threw a polaroid picture in front of him. 'It was taken by someone who was at the scene.' Grandma leant across his desk, breathing heavily with emotion. There was Grandma's red Ferrari, her pride and joy, lying beneath a huge branch, its front crushed almost beyond recognition. 'Six weeks I'd had it. £72,000 it cost.'

'What a mess,' he said, really meaning it. 'You're lucky to be alive. I see it just missed the driver's seat.'

'Another two feet and the branch would have hit me. Wouldn't have had a chance. It only happened this morning. About two hours ago. I'd decided to have a day at Epsom races.' As if another thought struck her, she suddenly delved into her basket and, with a flourish, produced the broken remains of her umbrella. 'Look at that.'

'How did that happen? It doesn't look as though the inside of the car was damaged at all.'

'I broke it on the tree. Gave it a right wallop. Felt better for that too but I want the cost of a new one included in the claim.'

'Ah yes, the claim. Obviously you've got some losses but I expect your own insurance company will pick up the price of repairing the vehicle, or its value if it's a write-off.'

Grandma sat back and looked slightly shamefaced. 'I only had third party, not comprehensive.'

'So that £72,000 worth of sports car may now be written off and you've lost the lot unless I can get it back for you in a claim against the owner of the tree?'

'Oh dear! You'll have to make a claim. I couldn't afford the premium for comprehensive insurance. Ridiculous price. The insurers thought I was too old to

216

have this sort of car. Whipper-snappers, the lot of them.'

'Well, I hope it wasn't a false economy, because suing for damages caused by falling trees isn't easy.'

'Well, it wasn't my fault.'

'Whose tree was it? It looks as though it wasn't on the roadside. It seems to have come from that garden by the road.'

'It did. What's more, the tree belonged to one of your lot—William Torquil Ponder. I saw him just after it happened. He gave me his card. Here it is.'

'You're sure it was Mr Ponder? It wasn't one of his clients who wanted you to get in touch with Mr Ponder?'

'No. It was him all right. I recognized him from Wayne's description. Anyway, he said it was him.'

Paul Bright smiled thoughtfully. 'I see. Well, no doubt Mr Ponder has insurance against this type of thing. But that isn't the same as getting damages. His insurers will only pay if Mr Ponder was to blame for what happened.'

Grandma's right arm automatically moved into the chopping motion which she always used when brandishing her brolly. 'Of course he's to blame. Just get on and sue him.'

'Well I remember that you had some shares in British Telecom, didn't you? That ruled you out of legal aid last time. Have you still got them?'

'£15,000 worth. Don't worry about legal aid. Just get on with it. I'll pay if you want. I know all the rules. What I don't know is, can I go out and hire another Ferrari?'

'I don't recommend it. The cost of hiring one will be enormous. In theory, you're entitled to hire a vehicle similar to the one which was damaged until you

217

get a replacement or the original one is repaired, but insurance companies always argue like mad over this. You'd only had the Ferrari for six weeks and they'd argue that you'd made do with a Morris Minor for years. My advice is that I should get an engineer's report on the vehicle and find out whether it should be written off or not. Your duty is to mitigate your loss, which means keeping the claim to sensible figures, so a quick decision will be needed about whether or not to repair the car. In the meantime, I suggest you play safe and hire a Ford Escort . . .'

'Ford Escort!' Martha Henderson threw the words back at him in disbelief. 'Over my dead body. I'll settle for a Porsche. Yes, I'll hire a Porsche. That's a lot cheaper than a Ferrari.'

'All right,' said the solicitor slowly. 'You may get away with that. But you're taking a chance and you'll soon eat into that £15,000.'

'Oh, I've got far more than £15,000. I've got all my TSB and British Gas shares as well.'

'Well, if it all goes wrong, don't say I didn't warn you. If the Ferrari is written off, then I suggest that you buy a Porsche rather than hiring. You're in a real danger area. Even assuming that the judge accepts that it was reasonable to hire a Porsche whilst you are waiting for a decision about the Ferrari, you shouldn't forget that you may have no claim at all. Then all the hiring has been done at your own expense. Irrecoverable. Think about it carefully.'

Grandma looked thoughtful. 'I'll get a quick decision on the Ferrari. What claims can I make anyway?'

'The value of the car or the repair costs as a start, plus garage storage charges and the cost of the vehicle being towed in. The hiring charges or damages for loss of use of the vehicle. That's the basis.'

'Nervous shock?'

Paul Bright laughed. 'You don't seem very shocked to me. I'd need strong medical evidence. And remember —you must mitigate your loss, which means you've got to act sensibly.'

'Don't give me that. I always act sensibly. Let me be the judge of that. You just recover the money.'

His knuckles rapped, Paul Bright chanced his arm. 'It wasn't very sensible not insuring the car, was it? If I can't make a recovery against Mr Ponder's insurance, then you've lost £72,000. Falling tree claims are difficult. What's more, if the vehicle is written off, you will not get back £72,000. You'll be paid the second hand value, probably about £65,000.'

'Nonsense. Sue for £72,000. I've only just run it in.'

'I'm afraid you can't beat the law. Anyway, let's see. They might be able to repair the car. If they do that, you can sue for the cost of the repairs.'

Grandma's mouth pursed as if she were sucking a lemon. 'Even if the vehicle is repaired, it won't be as valuable, having been in an accident.'

'Most engineers will say that the vehicle is not worth any less. Indeed, in the case of an old car which has repairs done, it can be argued that the vehicle is better, because some of the old parts have been replaced with new ones.'

Grandma snorted. 'Just let them try that argument on me. I'll teach them.'

Paul Bright was about to respond but thought better of it. Even without the umbrella, Martha was still an awesome prospect. 'I'll get experts to look at the tree and to inspect the car. The main part of the tree is on Mr Ponder's property and we'll need his consent. It's very still today. I wonder if the branch was weakened in that gale a few weeks ago? Anyway, that's for the experts. We have to prove that Mr Ponder was negligent in looking after his tree or, as the branch overhung the road, that the tree was a public nuisance.'

'Yes. Carry on,' said Grandma Henderson, scooping up the remains of her umbrella.

'Well it's quite good news. Although Mr Ponder's duty of care is similar whether we dress up the problem as nuisance or negligence, nuisance may be an easier route, excusing the pun. We only have to show that the tree was a public nuisance and that Mr Ponder caused it to enable us to pass the buck to *him* to show why he should *not* be held liable for breach of his duty of care. We have to prove less, you see.'

'Don't try and confuse me with hot air. I know you lawyers. All the same. Full of jargon just to put the fees up. Just get me my money. And don't forget, it'll be at least a tenner for a new brolly.'

Falling trees

Trees falling on the highway are a perpetual problem. The law books are littered with cases where innocent people have lost their claims, having failed to establish that the owner of the tree was liable, either for nuisance or negligence. Judges have taken the view that trees growing are a natural use of land and that it is not the duty of a house owner to have his trees regularly inspected by an expert. More may be expected of someone with a clump of trees by a road, but normally the test is that the owner of the tree can escape liability if it is not fairly evident to the average person that the tree is dead or decaying and represents a danger.

Many people have heard of the expression 'Act of God' as a defence. If a tree falls in an extraordinary gale (such as that of October 1987), it may be open to insurers to argue that the force of the gale/hurricane was such as to amount to an Act of God, which is a defence to an allegation that the owner of a tree was in breach of duty.

The important practical point is to get expert evidence about the tree, showing why it fell, as soon as possible, or at least to get photographs immediately after the accident. Otherwise, proving a case is exceedingly difficult. Though Grandma Henderson escaped injury (what tree would dare fall on her?) the law would be just the same if she were seeking damages for personal injuries sustained.

Henderson
V
Ponder

In which Mr Ponder is all at sea

'Anyone ever heard of Hedge, Fudgitt and Ponder, solicitors in Croydon?' asked the senior clerk of counsels' chambers in the Temple.

No one had. 'Why do you ask?' responded his junior clerk.

'Because I think they might be slightly mad. They've just sent a brief for Mr Horatio Greenhorn. No one's done that for twelve months. And the last firm are still regretting it.' The senior clerk shook his head in bewilderment.

The chambers in King's Bench Walk were one of the leading sets for barristers specialising in shipping law. There was scarcely a collision at sea or a mysterious sinking which did not bring solicitors hotfoot for the best advice in London. Hotfoot, that is, except for the benefit of the wisdom of Mr Horatio Greenhorn. In seven years at the Bar he had only received two briefs, but every day he came into chambers, living in hope that someone would recognise the true brilliance of his style, appreciate the cool forensic analysis which was his brain in top gear. 'So what's this case about in Croydon? A couple of rowing boats colliding on the lake in the park?'

'Far more important than that. I think we should show some respect for Mr Horatio Greenhorn. He's been briefed to appear on behalf of insurers over a falling tree.' The last words were almost lost in hoots of derisive laughter from all corners of the room.

'Heart of oak he's got, anyway,' someone suggested.

'Green fingers,' added another.

The senior clerk put the brief in the dusty space of Mr Greenhorn's pigeon-hole. 'Well, he's certainly green.' He shook his head in disbelief. 'But we still don't know any more about Hedge, Fudgitt and Ponder.'

Two days later, in the upper corridor of the Royal Courts of Justice in the Strand, Mr Ponder was having a word with his insurers. 'Oh yes,' he said breezily, 'I've got Mr Horatio Greenhorn. He really is the top man.' He mopped his brow with a spotted hanky and then blew his nose with resonance.

Mr Ponder's insurers were uncertain, but the claims manager looked reassured. 'I'm glad about that.' Inwardly he was regretting that his company had ever been persuaded by Mr Ponder that it was an insult to place instructions with another firm of solicitors. Normally the prospect of sending work to Mr Ponder would have sent the claims manager into a fit of apoplexy.

'Horatio Greenhorn was particularly recommended to me. What's more, I knew I'd made the right choice when I spoke to Mr Greenhorn's clerk yesterday. He assured me that Mr Greenhorn is really mustard. Just you wait and see.'

'Speaking of that, where is he?' enquired the claims manager.

'He's just putting his robes on.'

Down in the robing room, Horatio Greenhorn struggled into his gown and collar. It was an unusual experience for him, dressing up. Normally, he spent his time struggling to get 1 Down in *The Times* crossword. He never got any further. But at least it meant that he didn't have to dress up like this. Looking cautiously over his shoulder, he pulled out a half bottle of rum and took a generous swig. It was an old naval tradition which, even if now abandoned by the Navy, he kept alive and well in London EC4.

Meanwhile, up in the court corridor, Paul Bright was talking to Jeremy Sprigg with Martha Henderson by his side. 'You're in for quite a tough time,' warned

Paul Bright as he talked to Grandma Henderson. 'They've briefed a top barrister, Horatio Greenhorn. I've come across him before. In cross-examination he's without mercy and yet he is very popular with the judges too.' He turned to Sprigg, neatly attired in his wig and gown and ready for action. 'Have you seen Mr Greenhorn?'

Sprigg shook his head. 'Not today. In fact, down in the robing room there was only some old soak swigging rum from a bottle.' He stopped in mid tracks and then broke into a whisper. 'That's the chap I was talking about. He's just gone over to Mr Ponder. Whoever he is, it's not Horatio Greenhorn.'

'Find out who he is then,' snapped Martha. 'What am I paying you for?'

'Good idea,' said Sprigg and casually crossed the corridor to the group round Ponder.

'Excuse me,' opened Jeremy Sprigg, 'but I'm looking for Mr Greenhorn.'

Horatio Greenhorn spun round. 'Ah! You'll be Sprigg, won't you. I saw your name on the pleadings.'

Sprigg was taken aback. 'I'm sorry I didn't recognise you. You are Horatio Greenhorn?'

The other barrister puffed up his chest. 'Indeed I am. Now, if you have any particular points you wish to agree, no doubt we can have a word but otherwise, what I say is may the best man win. And I'm sure it's going to be me.' He burst into a guffaw of laughter whilst Jeremy Sprigg turned and, looking exceedingly puzzled, returned to Paul Bright. 'That chap *says* his name is Horatio Greenhorn. Just ring my clerk, can you please. See if he can explain the position.'

A few moments later Paul returned from making the telephone call. The grin on his face was wide. 'You'll never believe it! There are two Horatio

225

Greenhorns. The one we all know, love and respect is at Leeds Crown Court today. The one who's turned up comes from a set of shipping chambers. His nickname is Tugboat Annie.' He broke into a laugh. 'Mr Ponder has chosen the wrong one.'

It was the first time that Sprigg had seen Martha laugh. It was a rare experience and none the less pleasurable. 'That's what results from a solicitor with the wrong experience going to counsel.'

At 10.30 precisely the case was called, and, with no sign of any offer of settlement from Mr Ponder's insurers, the trial commenced before Mr Justice Beech. 'He's a good judge,' Jeremy Sprigg had confided, 'but he's not known for his sense of humour. I for one am certainly not going to crack any jokes about his name being appropriate.'

Not so Mr Horatio Greenhorn, who took the earliest possible opportunity to ingratiate himself with the court. 'It is most appropriate that the listing officer should have given us your Lordship in a case involving a beech tree.'

The Judge scowled. 'Yes, thank you Mr Greenhorn. I expected that you might say that and, just so that we can get rid of the puns for the day, may I tell you that my father was a police officer and was widely known as Copper Beech. Now, if we can please get on, I'd like to finish this case today.'

'Copper Beech!' repeated Mr. Greenhorn with a guffaw. 'Very droll, your Lordship, very droll.'

Jeremy Sprigg turned round and winked at his instructing solicitor. 'I think we're one-nil up already.' Then he was on his feet, explaining to the judge the background to the huge branch falling on the red Ferrari. He kept his opening short and then, in accordance with routine, called Martha Henderson, who was treated with every courtesy by the judge, offered a glass of water and the chance to sit down in the witness box. This she declined, giving her evidence with her hands gripped to the edge of the box, her body invisible and only her head showing.

She proved to be a good witness, keeping her answers short and, in reality, there was nothing for Mr Greenhorn to challenge. But he did. He wanted to prove that, in her Ferrari, Grandma Henderson had a chance of avoiding the tree. This was his moment, his chance to prove himself to a sceptical world. With all the experience of two shipping cases behind him, he rose to his feet and faced the withering stare of Martha Henderson.

'How fast were you steaming . . . going in your vessel?' he enquired.

'I was doing about thirty. No more than that.'

'Thirty knots,' said Greenhorn. 'I'm sorry, your Lordship, miles per hour. In such a powerful vessel, you should have had no trouble in taking evasive action—a mere touch on the tiller.'

'Rubbish,' said Grandma. 'I had no chance.'

'I must put it to you again,' said Greenhorn, 'that when this mast . . . er . . . tree started to topple, you had plenty of opportunity to steer to port to avoid a collision.'

'I had no time to swerve.'

'You could have dropped anchor. Pulled up pretty smartish?' prompted the barrister.

Grandma had had enough of this. A clenched fist appeared and she shook it at him. 'You weren't there. What do you know about it? I'm telling you, I couldn't stop.'

Greenhorn was unabashed. 'Was your vessel struck on the bow or the stern?' He looked at his papers again. 'Ah yes, it was the bow, wasn't it?'

Grandma looked confused. Mr Justice Beech leaned forward and addressed the barrister. 'Mr Greenhorn. I have not stopped you before, but it would help me and it would help the witness if you would carry out your cross-examination in language which we can all understand. I am aware that you are a member of the Admiralty Bar. Can I just say that you can regard the warning cones as having been hoisted.'

Greenhorn bowed slightly towards the Bench. 'I shall not turn a blind eye to that remark. Message received and understood, your Lordship. I have no further questions of this witness.'

Jeremy Sprigg then called Joan Wisley, who confirmed that she was a tree specialist. She told the judge that beech trees were susceptible to rot and fungal attack and that this particular tree, because it had multiple trunks, was one which needed regular inspection, particularly when some of the massive branches hung out over a busy highway. Photographs taken on the day that the tree fell showed obvious signs of scarring tissue plainly visible and a warning signal to laymen and experts alike.

'And what is that growing up the tree? I'm looking at photograph No. 7,' said Jeremy Sprigg.

The witness glanced at the photo. 'That is ivy. The tree was heavily covered in ivy and this adds to the danger of infection.'

'In your opinion, should a layman like the defendant, Mr Ponder, have recognised the dangers in this tree?'

'Undoubtedly. Of course an expert would have realised at a glance. A layman, however, on applying his mind to the situation, having looked at it, could see the tree was in an unsafe condition. There is no doubt in my mind about that.'

'I think that's a convenient moment for the adjournment,' said Mr Justice Beech. 'We'll leave cross-examination until 2.15.'

Outside the courtroom, Paul Bright congratulated Grandma on her evidence before turning to the barrister. 'So, Jeremy, I thought our expert came over very well.'

'I agree. But the big problem with the case remains that the judge is perfectly able to find that the average careful layman would not have looked at the tree. If you remember, there had been a serious storm less than a month before, with winds up to nearly 70 miles an hour. If the tree withstood that, if you had been Mr Ponder, you might well be reassured that, if your tree got through that storm, then there would be nothing to worry about. Anyway, let's see how Admiral Horatio Greenhorn gets on this afternoon.'

An hour later, Mr Greenhorn rose to cross-examine, suitably fortified by several more tots of rum and a pork pie from The George, over the road. 'Would you agree, Miss Wisley, that there had been a most serious gale twenty-seven days before the incident occurred?'

'Yes.'

'Now, I have here the shipping forecast for that day . . .'

Mr Justice Beech intervened. 'Do you mean weather report, Mr Greenhorn? You really must not confuse the witness by referring to shipping forecasts in a case like this. We are dealing with Croydon and not Cromarty.'

'If your Lordship pleases, I apologise. I am so heavily engaged in the Admiralty Division.' He beamed a cherubic smile at both judge and witness whilst, behind him, the claims manager was not sure whether he wanted to throttle Mr Ponder first before setting about Mr Greenhorn, or the other way round. His twenty years experience told him that this was going to be an expensive disaster, despite the fact that the case was easily winnable. He glanced sideways at Mr Ponder, whose eyes were heavy with sleep after an excellent steak and kidney pie and rice pudding.

Heads would certainly roll, the claims manager decided, his own being high on the list. His thoughts drifted back to the present where Mr Greenhorn was debating the subject of wind with the witness.

'This wind, Miss Wisley. Gusting up to 70 miles an hour. As this tree had withstood that gale, this would be most reassuring for Mr Ponder. He would be entitled to assume that there was no need for him to worry about it?'

'I think that if he had been reasonably careful, he would have gone round his garden to check. If he had done so, he'd have seen that it was a miracle that it had survived that gale and that his luck was soon going to run out. The tree had been flawed for a long time.'

Jeremy Sprigg turned to whisper to his solicitor. 'You won't get a better anwer than that. I don't think I want to re-examine. Greenhorn hasn't made any dents in the evidence. Agreed?'

'Aye, aye, Cap'n,' whispered Paul Bright in response.

'No re-examination,' said Jeremy Sprigg. 'That is my case.'

'M'lud,' said Mr Greenhorn, 'I shall now call Mr Ponder. He is my only witness. There is no real issue about the condition of the . . . er . . . branch before it fell. The issue is whether Mr Ponder was in breach of his duty of care, either in nuisance or negligence. That is my interpretation of this er . . . *branch* of the law.'

The judge ignored the pun. 'I understand,' replied Mr Justice Beech. 'How you go about defending the case is entirely a matter for you.'

Mr Greenhorn laughed loudly, an open mouthed guffaw, which reverberated round the room. 'Very droll, your Lordship, very droll.'

The judge looked puzzled. 'I don't understand Mr Greenhorn. Have I said something funny? Do get on with it.'

'Go about, your Lordship. Your Lordship was jesting, pulling my leg, talking to me in my own language, the language of the sea. Going about. It's a nautical term.'

The judge scowled. 'I do assure you, Mr Greenhorn, no pun was intended,' he said testily.

Mr Ponder waddled towards the witness box. It was a new experience for him and not one he relished despite the fortification of some red wine at lunch. Somehow he got through the oath and the first few questions from Horatio Greenhorn. But then suddenly, and perhaps inevitably, given the combined ability of Messrs Ponder and Greenhorn, the defence fell apart in just a few short seconds. It all started well enough with a question from Mr Greenhorn.

'Do you know how old the beech tree is?'

'I'm told it's been standing in the corner of our garden for 150 years.'

'Have you ever had it inspected?'

Mr Ponder nodded his head in agreement, his various chins rising and falling as he did so. 'Yes. It was inspected 25 years ago. It was all right then. That's when I bought the house.'

'And have you ever looked at the tree subsequently?'

'Not in the sense of looking at it as you mean. I see

it from the house. I'm a busy man, a very busy man. An endless stream of clients to help. I have better things to do than to go round my garden looking at trees.' It was a tactless, guileless response.

'So you would not have noticed a crow's nest, would you?' he chuckled, oblivious of the wrath of Mr Justice Beech. He continued. 'You've heard me describe the gale which took place a few weeks before this huge branch fell on a still day. You remember that gale?'

'Yes. Most alarming.'

'And what were your thoughts after that storm?'

'That the trees in my garden had all stood up to it very well and were obviously in good shape.'

Jeremy Sprigg noted the answers, which had been a mixture of good and bad from his client's viewpoint. He looked at his opponent, expecting Horatio Greenhorn to sit down and to leave Mr Ponder ready for cross-examination. It was the logical moment to stop but Greenhorn blundered on. And blunder it was.

'So you had no reason whatsoever even to consider inspecting that tree after the gale?'

It was one question too many and it put Mr Ponder on the spot. He was an honest man, but with little brain. He looked perplexed, wondering what to say next. 'Well yes I did have reason to inspect it. You see, after the gale, I had a circular letter from some tree experts, touting for business. They wrote saying that they had been passing the property and had noticed the scarring on the tree and had seen evidence of fungus. On their circular letter they put a particular note that the tree was in danger.'

There was an ominous silence in the room as the judge made his note. Then Jeremy Sprigg jumped up. 'M'Lud, it has to be said that this answer comes as a complete surprise to me. We have had discovery of documents in this case and yet here, for the first time, we all learn from Mr Ponder, who is a solicitor of the Supreme Court and experienced in these matters, that he had a letter, a fundamentally important letter, which has never been disclosed as part of the procedure. Your Lordship will understand that I must insist upon seeing this document at once. Furthermore, I would suggest to my learned friend, with the greatest respect, that, if the letter does give the plain warning which Mr Ponder has explained, then this is a case which might benefit from a short adjournment whilst his client decides whether or not he can contest it any further.'

The judge was quick to agree. 'What do you say about that Mr Greenhorn? Have you seen this letter? If you have, then I shall take a most serious view of the fact that it has not been disclosed.'

'M'Lud. No. The semaphore between solicitor and counsel has broken down. I was unaware of this letter. But strange things happen at sea.'

Mr Justice Beech snorted his irritation and then turned to Mr Ponder. 'Mr Ponder. Do you have this letter?'

'Why yes. It'll be in my briefcase. Shall I get it?'

'You'd better.' The judge wrote on his pad with heavy, forceful strokes of the pen whilst Mr Ponder rummaged amongst the digestive biscuits and will forms in his briefcase to seek out the vital letter. Then it was back to the witness box, where he stood whilst the two barristers studied the document and then handed it to the judge. 'Mr Ponder,' said Mr Justice Beech. 'This is a fundamentally important letter. It goes to the very root . . . I mean, core of the case. You're a most experienced solicitor, a senior member of the profession. Why was it not produced? You know the rules regarding discovery of documents?'

Once again Mr Ponder was flummoxed. Should he admit that he had never read the Rules of the Supreme Court in years? Certainly the concealment had not been deliberate. 'M'Lud, whilst I do get involved in some High Court litigation from time to time, my expertise lies in conveyancing and wills. I have some recollection of the law of discovery from when I was an articled clerk. But that was many years ago. I was under the impression that, as the letter was from an expert, it was privileged and therefore confidential.'

'Privileged! Confidential?' The wizened face of Mr Justice Beech creased in anger. 'For a solicitor of your experience, to have to admit to such incompetence! This vital document cannot possibly have the benefit of confidentiality. It existed before the litigation and should have been included in your list of documents and, if I may say so, it should have been given to your insurers, who, I am sure, would not have contested this case before me today, had they known of it.' The judge permitted himself a glance towards the man he'd identified as the insurer and was rewarded with a sharp nod of the head. 'I agree with Mr Sprigg that there be a short adjournment whilst the parties consider their position.'

'What a bit of luck,' murmured Paul Bright. 'If old Greenhorn had not asked one question too many, we'd never have found out about that letter and the judge might well have downed us on the evidence. It was still wide open.'

'I agree. I thought Ponder had acted no differently regarding the tree than anyone else would have done. But, of course, once he'd had that most blatant warning, he should have done something about it. Even now, he could tell the court that he had intended to act on the warning but hadn't had time. There's authority

234

in his favour on that proposition. But looking at them, I'd say the other side are now so demoralized that we'll probably get a deal. I'll have a word with them.'

Sprigg beckoned Horatio Greenhorn to join him and they put together agreed terms of settlement. 'I want judgment for my client for the full value of her vehicle. It was, as you know, written off. It was only six weeks old and cost £72,000. I know I've suggested it's only worth £65,000 but, unless you consent to judgment for the full amount, I shall not settle. You can see the time now. I'll let the case run into another day. I shall also take instructions on referring the entire matter to The Law Society as it's an outrage that a solicitor should withhold a material document. The least that your side can do is to compensate the plaintiff to the full extent. So we'll settle for £72,000, being the actual cost of the vehicle, plus interest. Also, I want damages for her nervous shock.' Jeremy Sprigg knew that this was a try-on but he felt that the moment was right to pitch everything in. 'My client, because of her advancing years, and knowing of the length of time that this case would take to get to court, mitigated her loss by buying a second hand Porsche Turbo, at a cost of £20,000. Most reasonable I would say. That was nearly two years ago. She's therefore lost the interest on that money actually spent and I want that sum paid in full. Once she's got her damages, then the Porsche can be sold and we'll make no claim for the depreciation loss which she will suffer as a result.' He made no mention of the fact that the Ferrari would have been depreciating in a similar manner. 'I've got instructions now to settle for £93,000, including all those matters but, in addition, I've advised Mrs Henderson that she must seek indemnity costs. I know the normal rule is that my client would obtain standard costs but, as this entire fiasco has come about due to the fault of Mr Ponder, who is after all a solicitor, I expect the judge will order costs on an indemnity basis and, indeed, may well order Mr Ponder to pay the costs personally. There's the package. Take it or leave it.'

'Message received and understood. We're rather shipwrecked, aren't we? I'll discuss it with my crew.'

For nearly half an hour harsh words were exchanged between the claims manager and Mr Ponder. 'My company,' said the insurer, 'would not be in this predicament but for your mistakes.' He too could see that he had Mr Ponder pinned against the ropes. 'The other side are using the thumbscrews but, frankly, I would as well in their position. I suggest that my company pays the £65,000 for the car. You pay the balance of their demands up to £93,000, plus their costs.'

'I see.' Mr Ponder bit his moustache and blinked back his confusion. 'I've made a bit of a mess of this. I suppose I'd better do what you say.'

The court resumed and Mr Justice Beech entered judgment for Mrs Henderson for £93,000, including interest, with costs on an indemnity basis.

It was all over.

'You've done well,' said Paul Bright to Grandma Henderson as they emerged into the Strand.

'You think so?' said Grandma parrying her way through people on the pavement with a deft series of movements with her umbrella. 'I didn't hear Mr Sprigg ask the other side for the money for my new brolly. I do feel very let down about it.'

Postscript

It is not always possible for your solicitor to get the barrister of his first choice to represent you in court on the day. Uncertainty of trial dates, hearings going on longer or finishing sooner than expected, make it difficult for the clerk of the barristers' chambers to plan the diary. There is nothing more infuriating to solicitor or client than to find, at the last minute, that the brief for the big case has been passed to someone else. Nevertheless, the best chance of getting the barrister of your choice to court is by using the right solicitor.

A lazy/incompetent/inexperienced solicitor may well instruct a like-minded barrister who accepts inadequate instructions and who is prepared to present a case to the court when the papers are in disarray. In contrast, the best barristers do not wish to stand up in court with a brief which is a shambles. They value their reputation too much to have to present a badly prepared case to an unforgiving judge.

We have seen here how Mr Ponder ran into trouble because he made the very silly mistake of sending the papers to the wrong barrister. It may seem extraordinary, but confusing two barristers with the same name (but very different abilities) has actually happened in real life.

Mr Ponder was finally hoist with his own petard because he failed to understand the significance of the letter from the firm of tree specialists; and he had forgotten the rules about disclosing documents to the other side.

The moral of this, the last of our stories, is therefore the same as the first: if you have to go to law, the greatest favour you can do yourself is to make sure you get the right solicitor.

And here we must leave the Hendersons—each of them all in one piece, at least for the moment . . .